W9-CLZ-364

Presented To:

_____

Presented By:

_____

Date:

_____

GOD'S Little Lessons on

Life

Honor Books
Tulsa, Oklahoma

Unless otherwise indicated, all Scripture quotations are taken from the *Holy Bible, New International Version* ®. NIV®. Copyright © 1973, 1978, 1984 by International Bible Society. Used by permission of Zondervan Publishing House. All rights reserved.

Verses marked TLB are taken from *The Living Bible,* copyright © 1971. Used by permission of Tyndale House Publishers, Inc., Wheaton, Illinois 60189. All rights reserved.

Scripture quotations marked KJV are taken from the *King James Version* of the Bible.

Scripture quotations marked RSV are taken from *The Revised Standard Version Bible,* copyright © 1946, Old Testament section copyright © 1952 by the Division of Christian Education of the Churches of Christ in the United States of America and is used by permission.

Scripture quotations marked NKJV are taken from *The New King James Version.* Copyright © 1979, 1980, 1982, 1994, Thomas Nelson, Inc.

Scripture quotations marked NAS are taken from the *New American Standard Bible.* Copyright © The Lockman Foundation 1960, 1962, 1963, 1968, 1971, 1972, 1973, 1975, 1977. Used by permission.

God's Little Lessons on Life
ISBN 1-56292-924-0
Copyright © 1998 by Honor Books
P.O. Box 55388
Tulsa, OK 74155

Printed in the United States of America. All rights reserved under International Copyright Law. Contents and/or cover may not be reproduced in whole or in part in any form without the express written consent of the Publisher.

Introduction

Life is filled with many challenging questions and situations. The good news is that real life answers are available right here in the pages that follow.

God's Word has all the direction and encouragement we need to face life with confidence and encouragement. The Bible is where we discover there are promises that apply to the areas of our lives that matter the most to us—from anger to forgiveness, from sorrow to joy, from marriage to friendship, and many more real life issues.

But more than a promise book, *God's Little Lessons on Life* presents a powerful devotional story to illustrate the scriptures that go with each topic. These life lessons are not just for knowing, but for living out day by day.

The promises of God are for you. He is always ready and willing to fulfill them in your life. Our prayer is that as you read through the pages of this book, you will discover all that God wants to do in and through your life.

Table of Contents

GOD's Little Lessons on Life concerning:

Anger

He who is slow to anger has great understanding,
But he who is quick-tempered exalts folly.

Proverbs 14:29 NAS

He that is slow to anger is better than the mighty;
and he that ruleth his spirit than he that taketh
a city.

Proverbs 16:32 KJV

Be ye angry, and sin not: let not the sun go down
upon your wrath.

Ephesians 4:26 KJV

If it is possible, as much as depends on you, live
peaceably with all men.

Romans 12:18 NKJV

Control or Be Controlled

A little girl was once in a very bad mood. She took her frustration out on her younger brother, at first just teasing him, but eventually punching him, pulling his hair, and kicking him in the shins. The boy could take it all and even deal back a few blows, until the kicking began. That hurt! He went crying to his mother, complaining about what his sister had done.

The mother came to the little girl and said, "Mary, why have you let Satan put it into your heart to pull your brother's hair and kick his shins?"

The little girl thought it over for a moment and then answered, "Well, Mother, maybe Satan did put it into my heart to pull Tommy's hair, but kicking his shins was my own idea."

Not all of the evil in the world comes directly from Satan. Much of it comes from the heart of man. What we do with our anger, hatred, and frustration is subject to our will. We can choose how we will respond to stress, or to the behavior of others. Our challenge is to govern our emotions; otherwise, they will rule in tyranny over us.

Anger

Wherefore, my beloved brethren, let every man be swift to hear, slow to speak, slow to wrath: For the wrath of man worketh not the righteousness of God.

James 1:19,20 KJV

A soft answer turneth away wrath: but grievous words stir up anger.

Proverbs 15:1 KJV

But now ye also put off all these; anger, wrath, malice, blasphemy, filthy communication out of your mouth.

Colossians 3:8 KJV

Cease from anger, and forsake wrath: fret not thyself in any wise to do evil.

Psalm 37:8 KJV

Starve Your Anger

General Horace Porter once wrote about a conversation he had with General Ulysses S. Grant one evening while they were sitting by a campfire. Porter noted, "General, it seems singular that you should have gone through all the rough and tumble of army service and frontier life, and have never been provoked into swearing. I have never heard you utter an oath."

Grant replied, "Well, somehow or other, I never learned to swear. When a boy, I seemed to have an aversion to it, and when I became a man I saw the folly of it. I have always noticed, too, that swearing helps to arouse a man's anger; and when a man flies into a passion his adversary who keeps cool always gets the better of him. In fact, I could never see the value of swearing. I think it is the case with many people who swear excessively that it is a mere habit . . . they do not mean to be profane; to say the least, it is a great waste of time."

Not only does anger give rise to harsh words, but harsh words feed anger. The seething soul uses up valuable inner energy, leaving far less for the normal healthy functioning of spirit, mind, and body. To rid yourself of feelings of anger and frustration, perhaps the first step is to watch your tongue!

Assurance

I, even I, am he who blots out your transgressions,
for my own sake, and remembers your sins no more.
Isaiah 43:25

As far as the east is from the west, so far has He
removed our transgressions from us.
Psalm 103:12 NKJV

For by grace you have been saved through faith;
and this is not your own doing, it is the gift
of God.
Ephesians 2:8 RSV

Let us draw near with a true heart in full assurance
of faith, having our hearts sprinkled from an evil
conscience and our bodies washed with pure water.
Hebrews 10:22 NKJV

Absolutely!

At age thirty-three, golfer Paul Azinger was at the top of his game. He had only one problem: a nagging pain in his right shoulder. After seeing the doctor, Paul received a call that changed his life. His doctor wanted him back in Los Angeles immediately for a biopsy. Paul forged a compromise: he'd do it as soon as he had played in the PGA Championship Tournament and the Ryder's Cup Challenge. He tried to convince himself he had tendonitis, but the pain grew worse. He had cancer.

Paul began chemotherapy. One morning while praying in his bedroom, he was wondering what would happen if he didn't get better. Suddenly the sun seemed to force its way through the blinds and a powerful feeling of peace swelled within him. He knew with absolute assurance that God was with him.

Two years later, Paul rejoined the pro tour, his cancer gone. He says that his main goal in life now has shifted from winning to helping people see that "God is there for them."

God is always with you. Even when your circumstances would make you believe otherwise, if you trust in Him, He will take care of you so that you too can tell others of His great compassion.

Assurance

All that the Father giveth me shall come to me; and him that cometh to me I will in no wise cast out.

John 6:37 KJV

And I am sure that God who began the good work within you will keep right on helping you grow in his grace until his task within you is finally finished.

Philippians 1:6 TLB

My sheep hear my voice, and I know them, and they follow me: And I give unto them eternal life; and they shall never perish, neither shall any man pluck them out of my hand.

John 10:27-28 KJV

If you confess with your mouth, "Jesus is Lord," and believe in your heart that God raised him from the dead, you will be saved.

Romans 10:9

Yes, Even These

Matthew was a tax collector, a hated man among the Jews for helping Rome tighten its occupation. Even so, Jesus loved Matthew and eventually chose him as one of His disciples.

Peter had a quick temper, his emotions easily triggered by circumstances. During the most critical hours of Jesus' life on earth, he denied knowing Jesus three times. Even so, Jesus loved Peter and empowered him to lead the early church.

Saul wreaked havoc on the church in Jerusalem, leading raids on the homes of Christians and imprisoning the devout. He consented to the death of Stephen, and was one of the official witnesses of his execution. He even requested letters of authority to extend the persecution of the church to other cities, including Damascus. Even so, Jesus loved Saul, appeared to him in a light from heaven, and called him to repentance.

No matter what a person may have done— no matter what their character flaws—Jesus loved them. He loved them to the point of dying on their behalf on the Cross. He died for your enemy, the friend or family member who has left you disappointed or frustrated. And He died for you.

Burdens

Do not be anxious about anything, but in everything, by prayer and petition, with thanksgiving, present your requests to God. And the peace of God, which transcends all understanding, will guard your hearts and your minds in Christ Jesus.

Philippians 4:6-7

The LORD preserveth the simple: I was brought low, and he helped me. Return unto thy rest, O my soul; for the LORD hath dealt bountifully with thee. For thou hast delivered my soul from death, mine eyes from tears, and my feet from falling.

Psalm 116:6-8 KJV

For I, the LORD your God, hold your right hand; it is I who say to you, "Fear not, I will help you."

Isaiah 41:13 RSV

These things I have spoken unto you, that in me ye might have peace. In the world ye shall have tribulation: but be of good cheer; I have overcome the world.

John 16:33 KJV

Good from A to Z

Rachel and Jim owned a commercial building, half of which Jim used for his dental practice. For fifteen years, they had encountered no difficulty in renting out the other half. Then they lost their renter. They counted on the extra income to pay their bills. A real estate agent told them, "Forget about advertising for a while. Absolutely no one is renting."

To ease her financial worries, Rachel started swimming laps at her local YMCA pool. One day when she was feeling especially anxious, she decided to pray as she swam, using the alphabet to keep track of the number of laps. She focused on adjectives that described God, starting with the letter A. By the time she had completed *twenty-six* laps, an hour had passed and her fears were gone. She knew God would provide.

A short time later, a physical therapist called to say she had seen the "For Rent" sign in the window and asked to see the office. It was exactly what she wanted, so she and her partner rented the space.

When you take your eyes off of your problems and focus on God and His incredible attributes, your worries will fade away. Remember, God's goodness stretches from A to Z!

Burdens

Cast thy burden upon the LORD, and he shall sustain thee.

Psalm 55:22 KJV

Come to me, all you who are weary and burdened, and I will give you rest. Take my yoke upon you and learn from me, for I am gentle and humble in heart, and you will find rest for your souls. For my yoke is easy and my burden is light.

Matthew 11:28-30

Humble yourselves, therefore, under God's mighty hand, that he may lift you up in due time. Cast all your anxiety on him because he cares for you.

I Peter 5:6-7

Carry each other's burdens, and in this way you will fulfill the law of Christ.

Galatians 6:2

The Worry Table

A military chaplain once drew up a "Worry Table" based upon the problems men and women had brought to him through his years of service. He found their worries fit into the following categories:

- Worries about things that never happened—40%
- Worries about past, unchangeable decisions—30%
- Worries about illness that never happened—12%
- Worries about adult children and friends (who were able to take care of themselves)—10%
- Worries about real problems—8%

According to his chart, 92% of all our worries are about things we can't control, things which are better left to God. The truth is, anxiety is rooted in a failure to trust God.

We simply don't believe He is big enough or cares enough to help with our problems, give us the desires of our hearts, and keep us—and our loved ones—from harm.

Once we know God's character, we can easily see how we worry for nothing most of the time. God is more than big enough, and cares more than enough to help us, bless us, and protect us. Give your worries to Him, and He will replace them with His peace.

Children

The promise is for you and your children and for all who are far off—for all whom the Lord our God will call.

Acts 2:39

But when Jesus saw what was happening he was very much displeased with his disciples and said to them, "Let the children come to me, for the Kingdom of God belongs to such as they. Don't send them away!"

Mark 10:14 TLB

Children are a gift from God; they are his reward. Children born to a young man are like sharp arrows to defend him. Happy is the man who has his quiver full of them. That man shall have the help he needs when arguing with his enemies.

Psalm 127:3-5 TLB

Only take heed to yourself, and diligently keep yourself, lest you forget the things your eyes have seen, and lest they depart from your heart all the days of your life. And teach them to your children and your grandchildren.

Deuteronomy 4:9 NKJV

The Wind Beneath Their Wings

When John was just a boy, he journeyed
with his family across the American continent. It
took the family a full year to make their way from
coast to coast. As each sunset and sunrise glorified
the sky, the Scottish father would take his children
out to show them the sky and speak to them
about how the cloud formations were surely "the
robes of God."

Who can fathom the full impact this trip
had on young John? Or how deeply rooted
became his reverence for nature on this year-long
journey? What we do know is that John Muir
became one of America's greatest naturalists. His
love for nature led him to the majestic mountains,
the glacial meadows, and eventually to the
icebound bays of Alaska. The lovely Muir Woods
in northern California are named in his honor.

What are you "showing" to your children
today? What "wind" are you putting under their
wings? What examples, what encouragement, what
insights are you giving to your child?

As the song declared so poignantly more
than two decades ago: "You are the wind beneath
my wings"—so is a parent's influence for each child.

Children

Train a child in the way he should go, and when he is old he will not turn from it.

Proverbs 22:6

He who spares the rod hates his son, but he who loves him is diligent to discipline him.

Proverbs 13:24 RSV

Discipline your son, for in that there is hope; do not be a willing party to his death.

Proverbs 19:18

The father of a righteous man has great joy; he who has a wise son delights in him.

Proverbs 23:24-25

Discipline Pays Off in the End

In *Dare to Discipline*, Dr. James Dobson tells about his own mother's approach to discipline: "I found her reasonable on most issues. If I was late coming home from school, I could just explain what had caused the delay. . . . If I didn't get my work done, we could sit down and come to some kind of agreement for future action. But there was one matter on which she was absolutely rigid: She did not tolerate 'sassiness.'"

He vividly recalls one particular spanking. He made the costly mistake of sassing his mother when the only object nearby for a spanking was her girdle. He says, "Now those were the days when a girdle was a weapon. It weighed about sixteen pounds and was lined with lead and steel . . . with a multitude of straps and buckles. . . . She gave me an entire thrashing with one massive blow!"

While Jim may not have appreciated her principles about discipline at the time, he certainly did in later years. His book, *The Strong-Willed Child*, is dedicated to her!

Disciplining our children shows them how much we love them. A child feels more secure and loved when he's been given boundaries and they're enforced.

Comfort

Blessed be the God and Father of our Lord Jesus Christ, the Father of mercies and God of all comfort; who comforts us in all our affliction so that we may be able to comfort those who are in any affliction with the comfort with which we ourselves are comforted by God.

2 Corinthians 1:3-4 NAS

But the Comforter, which is the Holy Ghost, whom the Father will send in my name, he shall teach you all things, and bring all things to your remembrance, whatsoever I have said unto you.

John 14:26 KJV

Don't be impatient. Wait for the Lord, and he will come and save you! Be brave, stouthearted and courageous. Yes, wait and he will help you.

Psalm 27:14 TLB

The LORD is good, a refuge in times of trouble. He cares for those who trust in him.

Nahum 1:7

Holy Comfort

In *Women Who Do Too Much*, Patricia Sprinkle writes:

> Three months before I spoke with Nancy, her husband lost a four-year battle to a degenerative brain disease. She said, "This was a brilliant man, a gentle man, a man with a terrific sense of humor. I grieved as he lost his ability to walk, pick up things from the floor, write, speak clearly. We had been married for thirty years and expected to grow old together. Suddenly, in one day, our life changed. He flew to Mayo Clinic one morning and called me that night with the doctor's diagnosis. They could do nothing for him.

> "I remember thinking after I hung up the phone, life is never going to be the same again. Nobody gets a rehearsal for this. You don't get to practice.

> "I was furious with God—banged my fist on many tables. But I learned to thank God that God is God. God didn't get bowled over by my fury. Instead, He told me, 'I won't leave you. I'm as sad about this as you are. I grieve with you.' The shared grief of God gets me through my own."

Jesus called the Holy Spirit the "Comforter." He alone is with us every moment of our lives.

Comfort

Come to me, all who labor and are heavy laden, and I will give you rest.

Matthew 11:28 RSV

The LORD is a stronghold for the oppressed, a stronghold in times of trouble.

Psalm 9:9 RSV

Though I am surrounded by troubles, you will bring me safely through them. You will clench your fist against my angry enemies! Your power will save me.

Psalm 138:7 TLB

Through the LORD's mercies we are not consumed, Because His compassions fail not. They are new every morning; Great is Your faithfulness. "The Lord is my portion," says my soul, "Therefore I hope in Him!"

Lamentations 3:22-24 NKJV

Talk to God

In the midst of her intense grief, Betty found it very difficult to pray. She was drowning in a sea of turbulent emotions and hardly knew her own name, much less what to request from God.

One afternoon, a friend of Betty's came by, and soon Betty was pouring out all of her hurts, fears, and struggles. She admitted she was angry with God and disappointed that her prayers for her husband's healing weren't answered. She admitted she was having difficulty believing God would do anything for her—in the present or the future. Finally, as the well of her emotions began to run dry, Betty's friend said quietly, "I have only one piece of advice to give you. Let's talk to God."

Betty's friend put her arms around her and prayed a simple, heartfelt prayer, claiming Christ's promise to heal her broken heart and restore her soul. After she had finished, she said, "Christ is with you. He is in you. And where He is, because of Who He is, He heals."

No matter what you may be going through today, your best recourse is to invite Jesus Christ to manifest Himself in you and through you. He knows the answer—He *is* the answer. He gives you Himself, and in Him is all the power, strength, encouragement, love, and comfort you need.

Conflict

I appeal to you, brethren, by the name of our Lord Jesus Christ, that all of you agree and that there be no dissensions among you, but that you be united in the same mind and the same judgment.

1 Corinthians 1:10 RSV

And the Lord's servant must not quarrel; instead, he must be kind to everyone, able to teach, not resentful.

2 Timothy 2:24

A wrathful man stirs up strife, but he who is slow to anger allays contention.

Proverbs 15:18 NKJV

See that no one repays another with evil for evil, but always seek after that which is good for one another and for all men.

1 Thessalonians 5:15 NAS

Hammering on Others

One of the most common expressions used to describe losing your temper is to "fly off the handle." This phrase refers to the head of a hammer coming loose from its handle as the carpenter attempts to use it. Several things can happen as a result:

- First, the hammer becomes useless—no longer good for work. When a person loses his temper, he often loses his effectiveness. Anything he says may not be taken seriously and is likely to be unproductive.

- Second, the hammerhead—twirling out of control—is likely to cause some type of damage to anything in its path. The person who loses his temper causes damage even if he doesn't realize it— perhaps physically to people or objects in his way, and nearly always emotionally to those who feel they are the victims of this uncontrolled wrath.

- Third, the repair of both the hammer and the resulting damage takes time. The person who loses his temper may recover quickly, but the victim of a hot temper rarely recovers as quickly.

So, as you can see, losing your temper is not the best way to handle conflict in life. Keep your temper today. Nobody else wants it.

Conflict

How good and pleasant it is when brothers live together in unity!

Psalm 133:1

May the God of steadfastness and encouragement grant you to live in such harmony with one another, in accord with Christ Jesus, that together you may with one voice glorify the God and Father of our Lord Jesus Christ.

Romans 15:5-6 RSV

Try always to be led along together by the Holy Spirit, and so be at peace with one another.

Ephesians 4:3 TLB

Don't grumble about each other, brothers. Are you yourselves above criticism? For see! The great Judge is coming.

James 5:9 TLB

The Tondelayo

In *The Fall of Fortresses,* Elmer Bendiner tells of a miracle that happened to him and a few others aboard their B-17 bomber, *The Tondelayo.* During a run over Kassel, Germany, the plane was barraged by Nazi antiaircraft guns. That in itself was not unusual, but on this particular flight the fuel tanks of the plane were hit. The following morning, the pilot Bohn Fawkes asked the crew chief for the shell as a souvenir of their unbelievable luck.

Bohn was told that not just one shell had been found in the gas tanks, but eleven!

The shells were sent to the armorers to be defused. Later they informed the Tondelayo crew that when they opened the shells, they found no explosive charge in any of them. One of the shells, however, contained a carefully rolled piece of paper. On it was scrawled in the Czech language: "This is all we can do for you now." The miracle had not been one of misfired shells, but of peace-loving hearts.

When we want peace in our lives, we must disarm our weapons—hurtful words, prideful looks, hurtful attitudes. When we diffuse conflict in favor of unity, God will flood our lives with His peace and love.

Courage

Be of good courage, and he shall strengthen your heart, all ye that hope in the LORD.

Psalm 31:24 KJV

Be strong and courageous, do not fear or be dismayed because of the king of Assyria, nor because of all the multitude which is with him; for the one with us is greater than the one with him.

2 Chronicles 32:7-8 NAS

Yes, be bold and strong! Banish fear and doubt! For remember, the Lord your God is with you wherever you go.

Joshua 1:9 TLB

Peace I leave with you; My peace I give to you; not as the world gives, do I give to you. Let not your heart be troubled, nor let it be fearful.

John 14:27 NAS

Speak Out and Stand Up

While he was a pastor in Indianapolis, Henry Ward Beecher preached a series of sermons about gambling and drunkenness. He soundly denounced the men of the community who profited by these sins.

The next week, Beecher was accosted on the street by a would-be assailant. Brandishing a pistol, the man demanded that Beecher make some kind of retraction about what he had said the previous Sunday.

"Take it back, right here!" he demanded with an oath, "or I will shoot you on the spot!"

Beecher calmly replied, "Shoot away!" The man was taken aback by his response. Beecher just walked away, saying over his shoulder as he left the scene, "I don't believe you can hit the mark as well as I did!"

Courage is more than just having convictions. It requires being willing to speak and to act in order to bring about change—in individual lives, in families, in neighborhoods, in cities, and in nations. It's not enough to "just believe" in something. In order to be a truly courageous person, you must be willing to speak out and stand up. Your voice can make a difference.

Courage

The Lord is my light and my salvation; whom shall I fear? When evil men come to destroy me, they will stumble and fall! Yes, though a mighty army marches against me, my heart shall know no fear! I am confident that God will save me.

Psalm 27:1-3 TLB

He gives power to the tired and worn out, and strength to the weak.

Isaiah 40:29 TLB

That is why we can say without any doubt or fear, "The Lord is my Helper and I am not afraid of anything that mere man can do to me."

Hebrews 13:6 TLB

Overwhelming victory is ours through Christ who loved us enough to die for us.

Romans 8:37 TLB

Be Strong and Courageous

Napoleon called Marshall Ney the bravest man he had ever known. Yet Ney's knees trembled so badly one morning before a battle, he had difficulty mounting his horse. When he was finally in the saddle, he shouted contemptuously down at his limbs, "Shake away, knees. You would shake worse than that if you knew where I am going to take you."

Courage is not a matter of not being afraid. It is a matter of taking action even when you are afraid!

Courage is more than sheer bravado—shouting, "I can do this!" and launching out with a "do-or-die" attitude over some reckless dare.

True courage is manifest when a person chooses to take a difficult or even dangerous course of action, simply because it is the right thing to do. Courage is looking beyond yourself to what is best for another.

The source of all courage is the Holy Spirit, our Comforter. It is His very nature to remain at our side, helping us. When we welcome Him into our lives and He compels us to do something, we can confidently trust He will be right there helping us accomplish whatever task He has called us to.

Death

He will swallow up death forever. The Sovereign LORD will wipe away the tears from all faces; he will remove the disgrace of his people from all the earth.

Isaiah 25:8

When calamity comes, the wicked are brought down, but even in death the righteous have a refuge.

Proverbs 14:32

I will ransom them from the power of the grave; I will redeem them from death.

Hosea 13:14 KJV

Whoever believes in Him should not perish but have eternal life.

John 3:15 NKJV

The Purpose of Life

J. C. Penney was well advanced in years before he fully committed his life to Jesus Christ. A good, honest man, in his early years he was primarily interested in becoming a success. His ambition was to one day be worth one hundred thousand dollars. When he reached that goal he felt temporary satisfaction, but soon set his sights on being worth a million dollars.

Both he and Mrs. Penney worked hard to expand their business, but one day Mrs. Penney caught a cold and developed pneumonia, which subsequently caused her death. "When she died," he recalled, "my world crashed about me. To build a business, to make a success in the eyes of men, to accumulate money—what was the purpose of life?" Before long, Penney was ruined financially. It was at that point that he turned to God. He said, "When I was brought to humility and the knowledge of dependence on God, sincerely and earnestly seeking God's aid, it was forthcoming, and a light illumined my being. I cannot otherwise describe it than to say that it changed me as a man."

Even in the midst of death, Jesus gives meaning and purpose to life. He brings calm to the storm and rest to the soul.

Death

But God will ransom my soul from the power of Sheol, for he will receive me.

Psalm 49:15 RSV

But the good man—what a different story! For the good man—the blameless, the upright, the man of peace—he has a wonderful future ahead of him. For him there is a happy ending.

Psalm 37:37 TLB

Since we, God's children, are human beings—made of flesh and blood—he became flesh and blood too by being born in human form; for only as a human being could he die and in dying break the power of the devil who had the power of death.

Hebrews 2:14 TLB

For to me, to live is Christ and to die is gain.

Philippians 1:21

An Upstretched Hand

Matthew Huffman, the son of missionaries in Salvador, Brazil, awoke one morning complaining of a fever. As his temperature soared, he began to lose his eyesight. His mother and father put him in the car and raced to the nearest hospital. As they drove, the boy lay in his mother's lap, listless. Then suddenly, he put one hand into the air. His mother took it gently and pulled it down to his body, but he extended it again. Again, she pulled it down. He reached into the air a third time. Confused at this unusual behavior, the mother asked her son, "What are you reaching for?" "I'm reaching for Jesus' hand," he answered.

With those words, Matthew closed his eyes and slid into a coma from which he never awakened. He died two days later, a victim of bacterial meningitis.

Matthew did not have a long life, but he learned the most important lesson a person can learn before he or she dies: He learned Whom to reach for in the hour of death.

Reaching for God is not only for the dying; it is for the living. In reaching for God's hand, we find the strength to live every day.

Deliverance

Because he cleaves to me in love, I will deliver him; I will protect him, because he knows my name. When he calls to me, I will answer him; I will be with him in trouble, I will rescue him and honor him.

Psalm 91:14-15 RSV

For he has rescued us out of the darkness and gloom of Satan's kingdom and brought us into the Kingdom of his dear Son.

Colossians 1:13 TLB

The Lord knoweth how to deliver the godly out of temptations, and to reserve the unjust unto the day of judgment to be punished.

2 Peter 2:9 KJV

Deliverance belongs to the LORD; thy blessing be upon thy people!

Psalm 3:8 RSV

Our Refuge and Strength

Norma Zimmer, a well-known singer for Lawrence Welk, had a difficult childhood. As a high school senior, Norma was invited to be a featured soloist at the University Christian Church in Seattle. When her parents heard she was going to sing a particular song, they both insisted on attending the service. She says about that morning, "I stole glances at the congregation, trying to find my parents . . . then in horror I saw them—weaving down the aisle in a state of disheveled intoxication. . . . I don't know how I ever got through that morning."

After she sang and took her seat, her cheeks burning from embarrassment, the pastor preached: "God is our refuge and strength, a tested help in time of trouble." She says, "I realized how desperate life in our family was without God, and that day I recommitted my life to Him . . . Jesus came into my life not only as Savior but for daily strength and direction."

God's deliverance is not only for the future, but for the present. He is an ever-present help in times of trouble. Daily rely on Him for deliverance and direction.

Deliverance

When the righteous cry for help, the LORD hears, and delivers them out of all their troubles.

Psalm 34:17 RSV

He who trusts in his own heart is a fool, But whoever walks wisely will be delivered.

Proverbs 28:26 NKJV

The Lord is my rock, my fortress and my deliverer.

2 Samuel 22:2

But I am poor and needy; Yet the Lord thinks upon me. You are my help and my deliverer; Do not delay, O my God.

Psalm 40:17 NKJV

The Thundering Legion

The Militine Legion was one of the two most famous legions in the Roman army. It was also known as the "Thundering Legion." The nickname was given by the philosopher-emperor, Marcus Aurelius in 176 AD., during a military campaign against the Germans.

In their march northward, the Romans were encircled by precipitous mountains which were occupied by their enemies. In addition, due to a drought, they were tormented by great thirst. Then a member of the Praetorian Guard informed the emperor that the Militine Legion was made up of Christians who believed in the power of prayer. Although he himself had been a great persecutor of the Church, the emperor said, "Let them pray then." The soldiers bowed on the ground and earnestly sought God to deliver them in the name of Jesus Christ.

They had scarcely risen from their knees when a great thunderstorm arose. The storm drove their enemies from their strongholds and into their arms, where they pleaded for mercy. The storm also provided water to drink and ended the drought. The emperor renamed them the "Thundering Legion," and subsequently abated some of his persecution of the Christians in Rome.

Let prayer be your first resort, instead of your last. Prayer and deliverance go hand in hand!

Discipline

But I keep under my body, and bring it into subjection: lest that by any means, when I have preached to others, I myself should be a castaway.

1 Corinthians 9:27 KJV

I have been crucified with Christ; it is no longer I who live, but Christ lives in me; and the life which I now live in the flesh I live by faith in the Son of God, who loved me and gave Himself for me.

Galatians 2:20 NKJV

He that hath no rule over his own spirit is like a city that is broken down, and without walls.

Proverbs 25:28 KJV

Let us walk properly, as in the day, not in revelry and drunkenness, not in lewdness and lust, not in strife and envy. But put on the Lord Jesus Christ, and make no provision for the flesh, to fulfill its lusts.

Romans 13:13-14 NKJV

From Catching Footballs to Flipping Burgers

In 1961, Jerry Richardson faced an important decision. As a wide receiver for the Baltimore Colts, he had a job that was considered glamorous and secure. But when the modest raise he had requested was turned down, he felt the time had come for him to take a risk and do what he had always wanted to do—he would start his own business.

Richardson and his family moved back to South Carolina, where an old college buddy invited him to buy into a hamburger stand. Richardson took the plunge and bought Hardee's first franchise. He went from catching footballs to flipping hamburgers twelve hours a day. After hours, he scrubbed stoves and mopped floors. His reward: $417 a month. Some would have thought, *It's time to punt.*

Tired and frustrated as he was, Richardson refused to give up. He employed the same discipline he had used on the football field to focus on making his restaurant more efficient, his employees the friendliest in town, and his prices affordable. Before long, his business boomed.

Today, Richardson heads one of the largest food-service companies in the United States, with $3.7 billion a year in sales. And he is part of an investment group that is seeking to purchase a new franchise: An NFL team!

God gives us the dreams and desires in our hearts. He will help us achieve them, but we must still apply discipline and diligence to get there. When it looks like you're not getting anywhere, turn up the heat and keep going. Hard work gets results!

Discipline

"I am with you and will save you," declares the LORD. "Though I completely destroy all the nations among which I scatter you, I will not completely destroy you. I will discipline you but only with justice."

Jeremiah 30:11

Blessed is the man whom God corrects; so do not despise the discipline of the Almighty.

Job 5:17

Blessed is the man whom Thou dost chasten, O LORD, and dost teach out of Thy Law.

Psalm 94:12 NAS

As many as I love, I rebuke and chasten. Therefore be zealous and repent.

Revelation 3:19 NKJV

Directed Discipline

A grandfather once found his grandson, Joey, jumping up and down in his playpen, crying at the top of his voice. When Joey saw his grandfather, he stretched out his chubby hands and cried all the louder, "Out, Gamba, out!"

Naturally, the grandfather reached down to lift Joey out of his predicament, but as he did, Joey's mother said, "No, Joey, you are being punished—so you must stay in your playpen."

The grandfather felt at a loss as to what to do. On the one hand, he knew he must comply with the mother's efforts to discipline her son. On the other hand, Joey's tears and uplifted hands tugged at his heart. Love found a way! If Gamba couldn't take his grandson out of the playpen, he could climb in and join him there!

Discipline, in its finest form, is "directing a child toward a better way." Discipline goes beyond punishment by instilling the desire never to repeat the misdeed, and instead, make a better choice. God's loving discipline toward us does just that. Through His Word and His gentle voice, He guides us toward a better way—His way.

Discontentment

All the days of the afflicted are evil, But he who is of a merry heart has a continual feast.

Proverbs 15:15 NKJV

Let not thine heart envy sinners: but be thou in the fear of the LORD all the day long. For surely there is an end; and thine expectation shall not be cut off.

Proverbs 23:17-18 KJV

Now godliness with contentment is great gain.

1 Timothy 6:6 NKJV

He who dwells in the shelter of the Most High will rest in the shadow of the Almighty.

Psalm 91:1

Money, Money, Money

In 1923, eight of the most powerful money magnates in the world gathered for a meeting at the Edgewater Beach Hotel in Chicago, Illinois. The combined resources and assets of these eight men tallied more than the U.S. Treasury that year. In the group were: Charles Schwab, president of a steel company; Richard Whitney, president of the New York Stock Exchange; and Arthur Cutton, a wheat speculator. Albert Fall was a presidential cabinet member, a personally wealthy man. Jesse Livermore was the greatest Wall Street "bear" in his generation. Leon Fraser was the president of the International Bank of Settlements, and Ivan Krueger headed the largest monopoly in the nation. An impressive gathering of financial eagles!

What happened to these men in later years? Schwab died penniless. Whitney served a life sentence in Sing Sing prison. Cutton became insolvent. Fall was pardoned from a federal prison so he might die at home. Fraser, Livermore, and Krueger committed suicide. Seven of these eight extremely rich men ended their lives with nothing.

Money is certainly not the answer to life's ills! Only God can give us peace, happiness, and joy. When we focus on God and His goodness, we can live content, knowing that God will meet all our needs.

Discontentment

Let your conversation be without covetousness; and be content with such things as ye have: for he hath said, I will never leave thee, nor forsake thee.

Hebrews 13:5 KJV

I have learned in whatever state I am, to be content: I know how to be abased, and I know how to abound. Everywhere and in all things I have learned both to be full and to be hungry, both to abound and to suffer need. I can do all things through Christ who strengthens me.

Philippians 4:11-13 NKJV

And we know that all things work together for good to them that love God, to them who are the called according to his purpose.

Romans 8:28 KJV

Not that we are sufficient of ourselves to think any thing as of ourselves; but our sufficiency is of God.

2 Corinthians 3:5 KJV

Contented Regardless

For decades, Grandpa had been stubborn and crabby. His wife, children, and grandchildren seemed unable to do anything that pleased him. As far as he was concerned, life was filled with nothing but bad times and big troubles. Eventually, his family expected nothing but a gruff growl from Grandpa.

Then overnight, Grandpa changed. Gentleness and optimism marked his new personality. Positive words and compliments poured from his lips. He could even be heard giving joyful praise to the Lord. One of the family members noted, "I think maybe Grandpa found religion." Another replied, "Maybe so, but maybe it's something else. I'm going to ask him what has happened." The young man went to his grandfather and said, "Gramps, what has caused you to change so suddenly?"

"Well, son," the old man replied, "I've been striving in the face of incredible problems all my life—and for what? The hope of a contented mind. It's done no good, nope, not one bit, so . . . I've decided to be content without it."

Never start counting your troubles until you've counted at least a hundred of your blessings. By that time, you will have long forgotten what your troubles even were!

Discouragement

Why are you downcast, O my soul? Why so
disturbed within me? Put your hope in God, for I
will yet praise him, my Savior and my God.
Psalm 43:5

Behold, the LORD thy God hath set the land
before thee: go up and possess it, as the LORD
God of thy fathers hath said unto thee; fear not,
neither be discouraged.
Deuteronomy 1:21 KJV

When I remember these things, I pour out my
soul within me. For I used to go with the
multitude; I went with them to the house of God,
With the voice of joy and praise, With a multitude
that kept a pilgrim feast.
Psalm 42:4 NKJV

Keep your eyes open for spiritual danger; stand
true to the Lord; act like men; be strong; and
whatever you do, do it with kindness and love.
1 Corinthians 16:13-14 TLB

Six Little Words—One Big Message

Sir Winston Churchill took three years getting through the eighth grade because he had trouble learning English. It is somewhat ironic that years later, Oxford University asked him to speak at its commencement exercises! He arrived for the event with his usual props—a cigar, a cane, and a top hat. As he approached the podium, the crowd rose in appreciative applause.

With great dignity, Churchill settled the crowd as he stood confidently before his admirers.

He then removed his cigar from his teeth and carefully placed his top hat on the lectern. Looking directly at the eager audience, with authority ringing in his voice, he cried, "Never give up!" Several hushed seconds passed. He rose to his toes and shouted again, "Never give up!"

His words thundered across the audience. A profound silence enveloped the crowd as Churchill reached for his hat and cigar, steadied himself with his cane, and descended the platform. His oration was finished.

Churchill's six-word commencement speech was no doubt the shortest and most eloquent address ever given at Oxford. His message was one every person present remembered for the rest of their lives.

No matter what obstacles you face in life, always remember Churchill's admonition: "Never give up!"

Discouragement

But Christ, God's faithful Son, is in complete
charge of God's house. And we Christians are
God's house—he lives in us!—if we keep up our
courage firm to the end, and our joy and our trust
in the Lord.

Hebrews 3:6 TLB

Being confident of this very thing, that he which
hath begun a good work in you will perform it
until the day of Jesus Christ.

Philippians 1:6 KJV

And we have confidence in the Lord concerning
you, both that you do and will do the things we
command you.

2 Thessalonians 3:4 NKJV

And so, dear brothers, now we may walk right
into the very Holy of Holies where God is,
because of the blood of Jesus.

Hebrews 10:19 TLB

An Audience with the King

Long ago, there was a band of minstrels who were not very financially successful. Times were hard and there was little money for common folk to spend on entertainment.

One night, the troupe met to discuss their plight. One said, "I see no reason for singing tonight. It's starting to snow. Who will venture out on a night like this?" Another said, "I agree. Last night we performed for only a handful. Fewer will come tonight."

Then an older man rose, and looking straight at the group as a whole, he said, "I know you are discouraged. I am too. It's not the fault of those who come that others do not. We will go on and we will do our best."

Heartened by his words, the minstrels went on with their show. Even though the audience was small, they had never performed better. After the concert, the old man called the troupe together. "Listen to this," he said as he began to read a note he held in his hand: 'Thank you for a beautiful performance.'" The note was signed simply, "Your King."

There are always at least two people who see what you do and how well you do it—you, and God.

Encouragement

But from everlasting to everlasting the LORD's love is with those who fear him, and his righteousness with their children's children—with those who keep his covenant and remember to obey his precepts.

Psalm 103:17-18

In the day when I cried thou answeredst me, and strengthenedst me with strength in my soul. Though I walk in the midst of trouble, thou wilt revive me.

Psalm 138:3,7 KJV

Be strong and of good courage, do not fear nor be afraid of them; for the LORD your God, He is the One who goes with you. He will not leave you nor forsake you.

Deuteronomy 31:6 NKJV

Trust in the Lord instead. Be kind and good to others; then you will live safely here in the land and prosper, feeding in safety. Be delighted with the Lord. Then he will give you all your heart's desires.

Psalm 37:3-4 TLB

Face Your Fear

In 1993, a deranged fan stabbed tennis star Monica Seles, narrowly missing her spinal cord. She recognized her assailant as a man she had seen loitering around her hotel, but she had no idea why he had attacked her. At the hospital, she couldn't stop asking, *What if he comes back?* That night, her parents and brother all stayed in her hospital room with her. Monica was assured that her attacker was in custody. Even so, she had flashbacks of his face, the blood-stained knife, and her own screams.

Six months after the attack, her assailant was given two years probation and set free. Her fear intensified, and she sought out a psychologist to help her. Encouraged by her peers, she made a decision to return to tennis. Then came yet another blow. A German judge upheld her assailant's suspended sentence, which had been appealed. She said to herself, *Monica, you have to move on.* Three months later, she played an exhibition match and scored two wins—one on the court, and one in her mind and heart.

Are you facing an obstacle that seems insurmountable? Be encouraged. The God Who never leaves you or forsakes you will be with you, strengthening you every step of the way.

Encouragement

But exhort one another daily, while it is called "Today," lest any of you be hardened through the deceitfulness of sin.

Hebrews 3:13 NKJV

Now go out and encourage your men.

2 Samuel 19:7

Judas and Silas, who themselves were prophets, said much to encourage and strengthen the brothers.

Acts 15:32

Preach the word, be urgent in season and out of season, convince, rebuke, and exhort, be unfailing in patience and in teaching.

2 Timothy 4:2 RSV

Change through Praise

In *Especially for a Woman,* Ann Kiemel Anderson writes in her unique style about her sister:

jan taught 3rd grade once. a long time ago. one bright-eyed boy would stand at her desk. watch her. talk to her. all the while wrapping his finger around a piece of her hair into a little curl. he thought jan was the shining star in the night. over & over, however, he did poorly in his work assignments & daily quizzes.

one day jan stopped, looked at him, & said, "rodney, you are very smart. you could be doing so well in school. in fact, you are one of my finest students. . . ." Before she could continue to tell him that he should be doing much better in school . . . he looked up at her with sober, large eyes:

"I did not know that!"

from that moment on, rodney began to change. his papers were neater. cleaner. his spelling improved. he was one of her top students. all because she affirmed him. she told him something no one ever had before. it changed his life.

Nobody ever became ill or died from receiving too much genuine praise and encouragement. Give an encouraging word today to someone who needs it. Remember, what you sow, you will also reap!

Failure

If the LORD delights in a man's way, he makes his steps firm; though he stumble, he will not fall, for the LORD upholds him with his hand.

Psalm 37:23-24

For whatever is born of God overcomes the world. And this is the victory that has overcome the world—our faith.

1 John 5:4 NKJV

Without counsel plans go wrong, but with many advisers they succeed.

Proverbs 15:22 RSV

The steadfast love of the LORD never ceases, his mercies never come to an end; they are new every morning; great is thy faithfulness.

Lamentations 3:22-23 RSV

From Struggling to Success

The difference between success and failure is often the ability to get up just one more time than you fall down!

Moses could have easily given up. He had an "interrupted" childhood, lived with a foster family, had a strong temper, a stammering tongue, and a crime record, but when God called him he said "yes."

Joshua had seen the promised land and then been forced to wander in the wilderness for forty years with cowards who didn't believe, as he did, that they could possess the land. He could have given up in discouragement, but he was willing to go when God said to go.

Peter had a hard time making the transition from fisherman to fisher of men. He sank while trying to walk on water, was strongly rebuked by Jesus for trying to tell Him what to do, and denied knowing Jesus in the very hour Jesus needed him most. He could have seen himself as a hopeless failure. But when the opportunity came to preach before thousands on the Day of Pentecost, he responded.

No matter what you've done, you're not a failure until you quit trying.

Failure

With God's help we shall do mighty things, for he will trample down our foes.

Psalm 60:12 TLB

If God is for us, who can be against us? He who did not spare his own Son, but gave him up for us all—how will he not also, along with him, graciously give us all things?

Romans 8:31-32

Now thanks be to God, who always leads us in triumph in Christ and through us diffuses the fragrance of His knowledge in every place.

2 Corinthians 2:14 NKJV

Lift up your eyes to the heavens, and look upon the earth beneath: for the heavens shall vanish away like smoke, and the earth shall wax old like a garment, and they that dwell therein shall die in like manner: but my salvation shall be for ever, and my righteousness shall not be abolished.

Isaiah 51:6 KJV

Lessons from Failures

Thomas Starzl became interested in transplants as a surgical resident in medical school. In 1958, he implanted new livers in dogs whose livers had been removed—all died within two days of the operation. A year later, he found a way to stabilize their circulation and the dogs lived for a week after transplant surgery. In March 1963, Dr. Starzl performed the first human liver transplant, but his patient bled to death. That failure, and a hepatitis epidemic that spread through artificial kidney and transplant centers worldwide during the early 1960s, forced him to abandon his liver program.

In 1968, Starzl and others reported the results of new transplant trials to the American Surgical Association. All seven children involved in the study had survived transplants, although four died within six months—an encouraging but not stellar result. By 1975, there were only two liver programs left in the world.

Then in May of 1981, Starzl and his team found success—nineteen of twenty-two patients lived for long periods after undergoing a transplant!

Starzl was criticized, even vilified, by the medical establishment for attempting liver transplantation, but he persevered. Today, liver transplants are routinely performed in hospitals around the world.

Let failures teach you, not stop you!

Faith

So now, since we have been made right in God's sight by faith in his promises, we can have real peace with him because of what Jesus Christ our Lord has done for us. For because of our faith, he has brought us into this place of highest privilege where we now stand, and we confidently and joyfully look forward to actually becoming all that God has had in mind for us to be.

Romans 5:1-2 TLB

They are justified by his grace as a gift, through the redemption which is in Christ Jesus, whom God put forward as an expiation by his blood, to be received by faith. This was to show God's righteousness, because in his divine forbearance he had passed over former sins.

Romans 3:24-25 RSV

But without faith it is impossible to please him: for he that cometh to God must believe that he is, and that he is a rewarder of them that diligently seek him.

Hebrews 11:6 KJV

For ye are all the children of God by faith in Christ Jesus.

Galatians 3:26 KJV

A Tug on the Line

A twelve-year-old boy accepted Jesus Christ as his personal Savior and Lord during a weekend revival meeting. The next week, his school friends questioned him about the experience.

"Did you hear God talk?" one asked.

"No," the boy said.

"Did you have a vision?" another asked.

"No," the boy replied.

"Well, how did you know it was God?" a third friend asked.

The boy thought for a moment and then said, "It's like when you catch a fish. You can't see the fish or hear the fish; you just feel him tugging on your line. I felt God tugging on my heart."

So often we try to figure out life by what we can see, hear, or experience with our other senses. We make calculated estimates and judgments based on empirical evidence. There's a level of truth, however, that cannot be perceived by the senses or measured objectively. It's at that level where faith abounds. It is our faith that compels us to believe, even when we cannot explain to others why or how. By our faith, we only know in Whom we trust. And that is sufficient.

Faith

What is faith? It is the confident assurance that something we want is going to happen. It is the certainty that what we hope for is waiting for us, even though we can not see it up ahead.

Hebrews 11:1 TLB

We live by faith, not by sight.

2 Corinthians 5:7

If you can believe, all things are possible to him who believes.

Mark 9:23 NKJV

And now just as you trusted Christ to save you, trust him, too, for each day's problems; live in vital union with him.

Colossians 2:6 TLB

Blind Faith

Dr. Amanda Whitworth was frustrated as she crept up a hill with eight cars in front of her. They were stuck behind a slow-moving truck, and she was in a hurry. Amanda's last patient had needed more attention than was allotted for regular examinations, and she was late leaving to pick up her daughter from day school. Now she breathed a prayer that she would not be late again. It would be her third time, and because the day school did not tolerate parental tardiness, she would have to make new arrangements for Allie's afternoon care.

Amanda silently fumed at the truck's progress. No one dared pass the truck, as it was impossible to see oncoming cars around it. Suddenly, the truck driver waved his hand indicating that all was clear ahead. As Amanda zipped past him, it occurred to her that this man was probably a stranger to all who passed him— yet nine people trusted their lives to this man.

What a tremendous picture of how we do all that we can do, and then we must trust even the smallest details of our lives to the care of God, our loving Heavenly Father. It's comforting to know that He can always see exactly what's ahead!

Family

A man must leave his father and mother when he
marries, so that he can be perfectly joined to his
wife, and the two shall be one.

Ephesians 5:31 TLB

Children, obey your parents in the Lord, for this
is right. Honor your father and mother (which is
the first commandment with a promise), that it
may be well with you, and that you may live long
on the earth.

Ephesians 6:1-3 NAS

Be very careful never to forget what you have seen
God doing for you. May his miracles have a deep
and permanent effect upon your lives! Tell your
children and your grandchildren about the
glorious miracles he did.

Deuteronomy 4:9 TLB

But if anyone does not provide for his own, and
especially for those of his household, he has
denied the faith, and is worse than an unbeliever.

1 Timothy 5:8 NAS

Raised in Love

"The family," says Mother Teresa, "is the place to learn Jesus. God has sent the family—together as husband and wife and children—to be His love."

In *Words to Love By*, Mother Teresa writes,

Once a lady came to me in great sorrow and told me that her daughter had lost her husband and a child. All the daughter's hatred had turned on the mother.

So I said, "Now you think a bit about the little things that your daughter liked when she was a child. Maybe flowers or a special food. Try to give her some of these things without looking for a return."

And she started doing some of these things, like putting the daughter's favorite flower on the table, or leaving a beautiful piece of cloth for her. And she did not look for a return from the daughter.

Several days later the daughter said, "Mommy, come. I love you. I want you."

By being reminded of the joy of childhood, the daughter reconnected with her family. She must have had a happy childhood to go back to the joy and happiness of her mother's love.

Today, think of some special ways to remind your family of your love for them; then put them into action!

Family

Do not speak evil of one another, brethren.

James 4:11 NKJV

If anyone says, "I love God," yet hates his brother, he is a liar. For anyone who does not love his brother, whom he has seen, cannot love God, whom he has not seen. And he has given us this command: Whoever loves God must also love his brother.

1 John 4:20-21

Behold, how good and how pleasant it is
For brothers to dwell together in unity!

Psalm 133:1 NAS

Both the one who makes men holy and those who are made holy are of the same family. So Jesus is not ashamed to call them brothers.

Hebrews 2:11

"You're Special!"

While on vacation in New England, Sue and Kevin purchased two red "You're Special" plates. They liked them so much they decided to use them as their everyday dishes. Then one day, one of the plates broke. Thereafter, Sue and Kevin vied nightly for the "You're Special" plate honors—not to receive the plate, but for the privilege of awarding it to the other!

When the plate finally broke, Sue said sadly, "I had never been affirmed as much in my entire life as I was those eight months that Kevin and I bestowed upon each other the 'You're Special' honors. What seemed like courtesy the first night Kevin gave me the plate actually set a precedent for our encouraging each other on a daily basis. We're looking for another set of plates now—including one for the baby that's on the way!"

There are many little things you can do every day to make your family feel special. Encouraging them on a daily basis sets a tone of warmth, peace, and comfort in your home. Think of ways to make each member of your family feel special today.

Favor

Never forget to be truthful and kind. Hold these virtues tightly. Write them deep within your heart. If you want favor with both God and man, and a reputation for good judgment and common sense, then trust the Lord completely; don't ever trust yourself. In everything you do, put God first, and he will direct you and crown your efforts with success.

Proverbs 3:3-6 TLB

For surely, O LORD, you bless the righteous; you surround them with your favor as with a shield.

Psalm 5:12

A good name is to be chosen rather than great riches, Loving favor rather than silver and gold.

Proverbs 22:1 NKJV

For whoever finds me [wisdom] finds life and wins approval from the Lord.

Proverbs 8:35 TLB

Kindness Returns

Many years ago, an elderly man and his wife entered the lobby of a small Philadelphia hotel. "Every guest room is taken," the clerk said, but then added, "I can't send a nice couple like you out into the rain, though. Would you be willing to sleep in my room?"

The next morning, the elderly man said to the clerk, "You are the kind of man who should be the boss of the best hotel in the United States. Maybe someday I'll build one for you." The clerk laughed and forgot about the incident. Two years later, however, he received a letter containing a round-trip ticket to New York and a request that he be the guest of the elderly couple.

Once in New York, the old man led the clerk to the corner of Fifth Avenue and Thirty-fourth Street, where he pointed to an incredible new building and declared, "That is the hotel I have just built for you to manage." The young man, George C. Boldt, accepted the offer of William Waldorf Astor to become the manager of the original Waldorf-Astoria Hotel.

When you go out of your way to help someone, you receive their favor, the favor of others, and—most importantly—the favor of God.

Favor

They did not conquer by their own strength and skill, but by your mighty power and because you smiled upon them and favored them.

Psalm 44:3 TLB

And Jesus grew in wisdom and stature, and in favor with God and men.

Luke 2:52

In his distress he sought the favor of the LORD his God and humbled himself greatly before the God of his fathers.

2 Chronicles 33:12

But God was with him and delivered him out of all his troubles, and gave him favor and wisdom in the presence of Pharaoh, king of Egypt; and he made him governor over Egypt and all his house.

Acts 7:9-10 NKJV

Qualified by Willingness

Although he was raised in church, Dwight was almost totally ignorant of the Bible when he moved to Boston to make his fortune. There, he began attending a Bible-preaching church. In April of 1855, a Sunday school teacher came to the store where Dwight worked. He simply and persuasively urged him to trust in the Lord Jesus. Dwight did, and a month later he applied to become a church member. One fact was obvious to all: Dwight knew little of the Scriptures. His Sunday school teacher later wrote, "I think the committee of the church seldom met an applicant for membership who seemed more unlikely ever to become a Christian of clear and decided views of gospel truth, still less to fill any space of public or extended usefulness." However, Dwight had favor with the committee. He was asked to undertake a year of study, which he did. At his second interview, his answers to the deacons were only slightly improved. He still was only barely literate, and his spoken grammar was atrocious.

Few would have thought God could ever use a person like Dwight. But God saw in the willingness of Dwight L. Moody all the raw material necessary to create a major spokesman for His Word. He had favor with God.

Fear

Fear thou not; for I am with thee: be not dismayed; for I am thy God: I will strengthen thee; yea, I will help thee; yea, I will uphold thee with the right hand of my righteousness.

Isaiah 41:10 KJV

Peace I leave with you; my peace I give you. I do not give to you as the world gives. Do not let your hearts be troubled and do not be afraid.

John 14:27

The LORD is my light and my salvation; Whom shall I fear? The LORD is the strength of my life; Of whom shall I be afraid?

Psalm 27:1 NKJV

But Jesus ignored their comments and said . . . "Don't be afraid. Just trust me."

Mark 5:36 TLB

Calm at the Core

In *Especially for a Woman,* Beverly LaHaye writes about how upset she was when her husband, Tim, told her he wanted to take flying lessons. Her immediate response was, "I think you're foolish! Why would you want to get into a plane with only one engine?"

Tim asked her to pray about the matter. He suggested, "Be open with the Lord. . . . Let Him know you're afraid of flying, but that you're willing to be changed if that's what He would have."

Beverly did just that. Tim took flying lessons, and she repeatedly committed her fears to the Lord.

Years later, she was a passenger in a commuter plane that was caught in a storm. As the plane bounced in the sky, the LaHaye's attorney—normally a very calm man—was sure they were going to crash. He looked over and saw that Beverly was asleep! He asked her later, "How could you sleep so peacefully?"

Beverly responded, "It had to be God. Only He could have brought me from that crippling fearfulness . . . to a place where I could fly through such a storm and be at peace."

The only way to truly overcome our fears is to commit them to the Lord. When we let go of our fears and let God deal with them, He can replace them with His peace.

Fear

Be anxious for nothing, but in everything by prayer and supplication, with thanksgiving, let your requests be made known to God; and the peace of God, which surpasses all understanding, will guard your hearts and minds through Christ Jesus.

Philippians 4:6-7 NKJV

But when I am afraid, I will put my confidence in you. Yes, I will trust the promises of God. And since I am trusting him, what can mere man do to me?

Psalm 56:3-4 TLB

Be not afraid of sudden fear, neither of the desolation of the wicked, when it cometh. For the LORD shall be thy confidence, and shall keep thy foot from being taken.

Proverbs 3:25-26 KJV

Even though I walk through the valley of the shadow of death, I will fear no evil, for you are with me; your rod and your staff, they comfort me.

Psalm 23:4

Calm and Collected

During the four-week siege of Tientsin, in June of 1900, Herbert Hoover helped erect barricades around the foreign compound and organized all the able-bodied men into a protective force to man them. Mrs. Hoover went to work, too—helping set up a hospital, taking her turn nursing the wounded, and serving tea every afternoon to those on sentry duty.

One afternoon, while she was sitting at home playing solitaire, a shell suddenly burst nearby, leaving a big hole in the backyard. A little later a second shell hit the road in front of the house. Then came a third shell. This one burst through one of the windows of the house and demolished a post by the staircase.

Several reporters covering the siege rushed into the living room to see if she was all right and found her sitting at the card table. "I don't seem to be winning this hand," she remarked coolly, "but that was the third shell and therefore the last one for the present anyway. Their pattern is three in a row. Let's go and have tea."

Staying calm in the face of danger is your best defense. Worrying about what *might* happen causes unnecessary stress. So relax, and remember you're in God's hands.

Finances

And God is able to make all grace abound to you, so that in all things at all times, having all that you need, you will abound in every good work.

2 Corinthians 9:8

"Bring the whole tithe into the storehouse, that there may be food in my house. Test me in this," says the Lord Almighty, "and see if I will not throw open the floodgates of heaven and pour out so much blessing that you will not have room enough for it."

Malachi 3:10

The silver is mine, and the gold is mine, says the LORD of hosts. The latter splendor of this house shall be greater than the former, says the LORD of hosts; and in this place I will give prosperity, says the LORD of hosts.

Haggai 2:8-9 RSV

Honor the Lord by giving him the first part of all your income, and he will fill your barns with wheat and barley and overflow your wine vats with the finest wines.

Proverbs 3:9-10 TLB

Reaping a Harvest

The late Spencer Penrose, whose brother was a major political leader in Philadelphia in the late nineteenth century, was considered the "black sheep" of the family. He chose to live in the West, instead of the East. In 1891, fresh out of Harvard, he made his way to Colorado Springs. Not long after his move, he wired his brother for $1,500 so that he might go into a mining venture. His brother telegraphed him $150 instead—enough for train fare home—and warned him against the deal.

Years later, Spencer returned to Philadelphia and handed his brother $75,000 in gold coins—payment, he said, for his "investment" in his mining operation. His brother was stunned. He had qualms about accepting the money, however, and reminded his brother that he had advised against the venture and had only given him $150. "That," replied Spencer, "is why I'm only giving you $75,000. If you had sent me the full $1,500 I requested, I would be giving you three-quarters of a million dollars."

Nothing invested, nothing gained. Every harvest requires an initial seed. Be generous in your seed-sowing. Plant in good ground, and you can anticipate a good return.

Finances

So we should be well satisfied without money if we have enough food and clothing.

1 Timothy 6:8 TLB

I know what it is to be in need, and I know what it is to have plenty. I have learned the secret of being content in any and every situation, whether well fed or hungry, whether living in plenty or in want.

Philippians 4:12

And it is he who will supply all your needs from his riches in glory, because of what Christ Jesus has done for us.

Philippians 4:19 TLB

For you know the grace of our Lord Jesus Christ, that though He was rich, yet for your sake He became poor, that you through His poverty might become rich.

2 Corinthians 8:9 NAS

Cattle for Sale

Soon after Dallas Theological Seminary opened in 1924, it faced a major financial crisis. Creditors banded together and announced that they intended to foreclose. On the morning of the threatened foreclosure, the leadership of the seminary met in the president's office to pray that God would meet their need. One of the men present was Harry Ironside, who prayed in his characteristic style, "Lord, the cattle on a thousand hills are Thine. Please sell some of them and send us the money."

While they were praying, a tall Texan walked into the outer office and said to the secretary, "I just sold two carloads of cattle. I've been trying to make a business deal but it fell through, and I feel compelled to give the money to the seminary. I don't know if you need it, but here's the check."

Knowing the financial need, the secretary took the check and timidly tapped on the door of the office where the prayer meeting was being held. When Dr. Chafer saw the check, he was amazed. The gift was *exactly* the amount of the debt! Recognizing the name on the check as that of a prominent Fort Worth cattleman, he announced with joy, "Harry, God sold the cattle!"

Forgiveness

In him we have redemption through his blood, the forgiveness of our trespasses, according to the riches of his grace which he lavished upon us.

Ephesians 1:7-8 RSV

As far as the east is from the west, so far has he removed our transgressions from us.

Psalm 103:12

You were dead in sins, and your sinful desires were not yet cut away. Then he gave you a share in the very life of Christ, for he forgave all your sins.

Colossians 2:13 TLB

If we confess our sins, He is faithful and just to forgive us our sins and to cleanse us from all unrighteousness.

1 John 1:9 NKJV

Forgiven and Forgotten

A much-loved minister of God once carried a secret burden of a long-past sin buried deep in his heart. He had committed the sin many years before. No one knew what he had done, but they did know he had repented. Even so, he had suffered years of remorse over the incident.

A woman in his church deeply loved God and claimed to have visions in which Jesus Christ spoke to her. The minister, skeptical of her claims, asked her, "The next time you speak to the Lord, would you please ask Him what sin your minister committed while he was in seminary." The woman agreed.

When she came to the church a few days later the minister asked, "Did He visit you?"

She said, "Yes."

"And did you ask Him what sin I committed in seminary?"

"Yes, I asked Him," she replied.

"Well, what did He say?"

"He said, 'I don't remember.'"

The forgiveness we receive in Christ is complete. As far as God is concerned, our sin is over with and forgotten. We must learn to rest in His forgiveness and release the guilt and shame of our sin. Then we can walk in the assurance of our salvation and experience God's rest and peace.

Forgiveness

Your heavenly Father will forgive you if you forgive those who sin against you.

Matthew 6:14 TLB

But I say: Love your enemies! Pray for those who persecute you! In that way you will be acting as true sons of your Father in heaven. For he gives his sunlight to both the evil and the good, and sends rain on the just and on the unjust too.

Matthew 5:44-45 TLB

And whenever you stand praying, forgive, if you have anything against anyone; so that your Father also who is in heaven may forgive you your transgressions.

Mark 11:25-26 NAS

If your enemy is hungry, feed him; if he is thirsty, give him drink; for by so doing you will heap burning coals upon his head.

Romans 12:20 RSV

Set Free

Years after her experience in a Nazi concentration camp, Corrie ten Boom found herself standing face to face with one of the most cruel and heartless German guards she had met while in the camps. This man had humiliated and degraded both her and her sister, jeering at them and visually "raping" them as they stood in the delousing shower.

Now he stood before her with an outstretched hand, asking, "Will you forgive me?" Corrie said:

> I stood there with coldness clutching at my heart, but I know that the will can function regardless of the temperature of the heart. I prayed, "Jesus, help me!" Woodenly, mechanically I thrust my hand into the one stretched out to me and I experienced an incredible thing. The current started in my shoulder, raced down into my arm and sprang into our clutched hands. Then this warm reconciliation seemed to flood my whole being, bringing tears to my eyes. "I forgive you, brother," I cried with my whole heart. For a long moment we grasped each other's hands, the former guard, the former prisoner. I have never known the love of God so intensely as I did in that moment!

When we forgive we set a prisoner free—ourselves!

Giving

Remember this: Whoever sows sparingly will also reap sparingly, and whoever sows generously will also reap generously. Each man should give what he has decided in his heart to give, not reluctantly or under compulsion, for God loves a cheerful giver. And God is able to make all grace abound to you, so that in all things at all times, having all that you need, you will abound in every good work.

2 Corinthians 9:6-8

In all things I have shown you that by so toiling one must help the weak, remembering the words of the Lord Jesus, how he said, "It is more blessed to give than to receive."

Acts 20:35 RSV

Yes, ascribe to the Lord The glory due his name! Bring an offering and come before him; Worship the Lord when clothed with holiness!

1 Chronicles 16:29 TLB

Whoever can be trusted with very little can also be trusted with much, and whoever is dishonest with very little will also be dishonest with much. So if you have not been trustworthy in handling worldly wealth, who will trust you with true riches?

Luke 16:10-11

Grateful Giving

The story is told of a man and woman who gave a sizable contribution to their church to honor the memory of their son, who lost his life in the war. When the generous donation was announced to the congregation, a woman whispered to her husband, "Let's give the same amount in honor of each of our boys."

The husband replied, "What are you talking about? Neither one of our sons was killed in the war."

"Exactly," said the woman. "Let's give it as an expression of our gratitude to God for sparing their lives!"

All of our charitable giving in life produces benefits in three ways:

1. It helps those in need,
2. It inspires others to give, and
3. It builds character in us—selflessness, temperance, generosity, and compassion.

Keep in mind that when you give, you are ultimately giving to people, even though your gift might be made to an institution or organization. Churches and other charitable organizations are comprised of people. Your giving not only brings sunshine to the lives of others but to your life as well.

Giving

On every Lord's Day each of you should put aside something from what you have earned during the week, and use it for this offering. The amount depends on how much the Lord has helped you earn.

1 Corinthians 16:2 TLB

Give, and it will be given to you. A good measure, pressed down, shaken together and running over, will be poured into your lap. For with the measure you use, it will be measured to you.

Luke 6:38

As soon as the order went out, the Israelites generously gave the firstfruits of their grain, new wine, oil and honey and all that the fields produced. They brought a great amount, a tithe of everything.

2 Chronicles 31:5

Every man shall give as he is able, according to the blessing of the LORD your God which he has given you.

Deuteronomy 16:17 RSV

Brotherly Love

Two brothers farmed together. Each day they met in the fields to work side-by-side. One brother married and had a large family. The other lived alone. Still, they divided the harvest from the fields equally.

One night the single brother thought, *My brother is struggling to support a large family, but I get half of the harvest.* With great love in his heart, he gathered a box of things he had purchased from his earnings. He planned to slip over to his brother's shed, unload the basket there, and never say a word about it.

That same night, the married brother thought, *My brother is alone. He doesn't know the joys of having a family.* Out of love, he decided to take over a basket with a quilt and homemade bread and preserves. He planned to leave the items on his porch and never say a word.

One of the greatest joys in life comes from giving to those in need. And we always have something to give: our time, our finances, our effort. Often, the very thing we take for granted may be a tremendous blessing to someone else. What do you have in your hand? Give, and it will be given to you!

Guidance

For this God is our God for ever and ever; he will be our guide even to the end.

Psalm 48:14

The steps of a good man are ordered by the LORD: and he delighteth in his way.

Psalm 37:23 KJV

Yet I am always with you; you hold me by my right hand. You guide me with your counsel, and afterward you will take me into glory.

Psalm 73:23-24

I will instruct you (says the Lord) and guide you along the best pathway for your life; I will advise you and watch your progress.

Psalm 32:8 TLB

The Guide

While skiing in Colorado one day, a man noticed some people on the slope wearing red vests. Moving closer, he could read these words on their vests: BLIND SKIER. He couldn't believe it. He had difficulty skiing with 20/20 vision! How could people without sight manage to ski?

He watched the skiers for awhile and discovered their secret. Each skier had a guide who skied beside, behind, or in front of him, always in a position where the two could easily communicate. The guide used two basic forms of communication. First, tapping his ski poles together to assure the blind person that he was there, and second, speaking simple, specific directions: "Go right. Turn left. Slow. Stop. Skier on your right."

The skier's responsibility was to trust the guide to give good instructions, and to immediately and completely obey those instructions.

We can't see even five seconds into the future. We cannot see the struggles to come. Other people may run into us, or we into them, like errant skiers on a crowded slope. But God has given us the Holy Spirit to be our Guide through life—to walk before and behind us, and to dwell in us. Our role is to listen and to obey.

Guidance

For all who are led by the Spirit of God are Sons of God.

Romans 8:14 RSV

Yea, thou art my rock and my fortress; for thy name's sake lead me and guide me.

Psalm 31:3 RSV

And the LORD will guide you continually, and satisfy your desire with good things, and make your bones strong; and you shall be like a watered garden, like a spring of water, whose waters fail not.

Isaiah 58:11 RSV

When the Holy Spirit, who is truth, comes, he shall guide you into all truth, for he will not be presenting his own ideas, but will be passing on to you what he has heard. He will tell you about the future.

John 16:13 TLB

Finding the Path

E. Stanley Jones tells the story of a missionary who became lost in an African jungle. Looking around, he saw nothing but bush and a few clearings. He stumbled about until he finally came across a native hut. He asked one of the natives if he could lead him out of the jungle and back to the mission station. The native agreed to help him.

"Thank you!" exclaimed the missionary. "Which way do I go?" The native replied, "Walk." And so they did, hacking their way through the unmarked jungle for more than an hour.

Pausing to rest, the missionary looked around and had the same overwhelming sense that he was lost. All he saw was bush, and a few clearings. "Are you quite sure this is the way?" he asked. "I don't see any path."

The native looked at him and replied, "Bwana, in this place there is no path. I am the path."

When we have no clues, we must remember that God Who guides us is omniscient—all wise. When we run out of time, we must remember that God is omnipresent—all time is in His hand. When we are weak, we must remember that God is omnipotent—all power belongs to Him.

Happiness

For to the man who pleases him God gives
wisdom and knowledge and joy.

Ecclesiastes 2:26 RSV

Daughter of Babylon . . . happy shall he be, that
rewardeth thee as thou hast served us.

Psalm 137:8 KJV

A glad heart makes a cheerful countenance, but by
sorrow of heart the spirit is broken.

Proverbs 15:13 RSV

Happiness or sadness or wealth should not keep
anyone from doing God's work.

1 Corinthians 7:30 TLB

The Happiest People on Earth

A newspaper in England once asked this question of its readers, "Who are the happiest people on the earth?"

The four prize-winning answers were:

- A little child building sand castles.
- A craftsman or artist whistling over a job well done.
- A mother, bathing her baby after a busy day.
- A doctor who has finished a difficult and dangerous operation that saved a human life.

The paper's editors were surprised to find virtually no one submitted kings, emperors, millionaires, or others of wealth and rank as the happiest people on earth.

W. Beran Wolfe once said:

If you observe a really happy man you will find him building a boat, writing a symphony, educating his son, growing double dahlias in his garden, or looking for dinosaur eggs in the Gobi desert. He will not be searching for happiness as if it were a collar button that has rolled under the radiator. He will not be striving for it as a goal in itself. He will have become aware that he is happy in the course of living life twenty-four crowded hours of the day.

Happiness

Be happy, young man, while you are young, and let your heart give you joy in the days of your youth.

Ecclesiastes 11:9

Rejoice in the Lord always. I will say it again: Rejoice!

Philippians 4:4

The desert and the parched land will be glad; the wilderness will rejoice and blossom. Like the crocus, it will burst into bloom; it will rejoice greatly and shout for joy.

Isaiah 35:1-2

And those who have reason to be thankful should continually be singing praises to the Lord.

James 5:13 TLB

The World Won't Make You Happy

When the great golfer Babe Didrikson Zaharias was dying of cancer, her husband George Zaharias came to her bedside. Although he desired to be strong for her sake, he found he was unable to control his emotions and began to cry. Babe said to him gently, "Now honey, don't take on so. While I've been in the hospital, I have learned one thing. A moment of happiness is a lifetime, and I have had a lot of happiness."

Happiness flows from within. It is found in the moments of life we label as "quality" rather than "quantity." It rises up in life's greatest tragedies when we choose to smile at what we know to be good and lasting, rather than to cry at what temporarily hurts us. George Bernard Shaw once said, "This is the true joy in life: Being used for a purpose recognized by yourself as a mighty one. . . . being a force of nature instead of a feverish, selfish, little clod of ailments and grievances, complaining that the world will not devote itself to making you happy."

The only person who can truly make you happy is yourself. You simply have to decide to be happy.

Health

Yes, I will bless the Lord and not forget the glorious things he does for me. He forgives all my sins. He heals me.

Psalm 103:2-3 TLB

Surely he took up our infirmities and carried our sorrows, yet we considered him stricken by God, smitten by him, and afflicted. But he was pierced for our transgressions, he was crushed for our iniquities; the punishment that brought us peace was upon him, and by his wounds we are healed.

Isaiah 53:4-5

And ye shall serve the LORD your God, and he shall bless thy bread, and thy water; and I will take sickness away from the midst of thee. There shall nothing cast their young, nor be barren, in thy land: the number of thy days I will fulfil.

Exodus 23:25-26 KJV

Heal me, O LORD, and I shall be healed; save me, and I shall be saved: for thou art my praise.

Jeremiah 17:14 KJV

Standing in the Gap

A young woman lay in a hospital, far from home and family, drifting in and out of consciousness. Several times she became aware of a woman's voice praying for her salvation, as well as for her physical healing. At one point, a physician described her condition as critical, warning those present in the room that she might not survive. Then she heard a second voice, one that spoke in faith: "Doctor, I respect what you say, but I cannot accept it. I've been praying and I believe she will not only recover, but she will walk out of here and live for God."

Before long, the young woman did walk out of that hospital and return to work. It was then she learned that it had been her boss' wife (whom she had met only twice) who had stood in the gap, interceding for her at her hospital bed. When she attempted to thank this woman for her prayers, she replied, "Don't thank me, thank God. Others have prayed for me. Their prayers changed my life."

It was five more years before she gave her life to Christ, but all the while, she never forgot how a faithful woman of God had believed He was faithful to heal.

Health

And all the crowd sought to touch him, for power came forth from him and healed them all.

Luke 6:19 RSV

Jesus went throughout Galilee, teaching in their synagogues, preaching the good news of the kingdom, and healing every disease and sickness among the people.

Matthew 4:23

Look! A leper is approaching. He kneels before him, worshipping. "Sir," the leper pleads, "if you want to, you can heal me." Jesus touches the man. "I want to," he says. "Be healed." And instantly the leprosy disappears.

Matthew 8:2-3 TLB

Is any one of you sick? He should call the elders of the church to pray over him and anoint him with oil in the name of the Lord. And the prayer offered in faith will make the sick person well; the Lord will raise him up. If he has sinned, he will be forgiven.

James 5:14-15

Lord, Be My Strength

Dr. A. B. Simpson, a New York preacher, was plagued by poor health. Two nervous breakdowns and a heart condition led a well-known New York physician to tell him—at the age of thirty-eight—that he would never live to be forty.

In desperation, Simpson went to the *Bible* to find out what Jesus had to say about disease. He became convinced that Jesus always meant for healing to be a part of redemption. One Friday afternoon shortly after Simpson came to this conclusion, he went for a walk in the country. Coming to a pine woods, he sat down on a log to rest and pray. He asked Christ to enter him and to become his physical strength until his life's work was accomplished. He later said, "Every fiber in me was tingling with the sense of God's presence."

Days later, Simpson climbed a 3,000-foot mountain. He said, "When I reached the top, the world of weakness and fear was lying at my feet. From that time on I literally had a new heart." He went on to preach 3,000 sermons in the next three years, holding as many as twenty meetings a week. He amassed an amazing volume of work before he died—at the age of seventy-six.

Hope

Behold, the eye of the LORD is upon them that fear him, upon them that hope in his mercy.

Psalm 33:18 KJV

It is good that a man should both hope and quietly wait for the salvation of the LORD.

Lamentations 3:26 KJV

Happy is he whose help is the God of Jacob, whose hope is in the LORD his God, who made heaven and earth, the sea, and all that is in them; who keeps faith for ever.

Psalm 146:5-6 RSV

Through him we have obtained access to this grace in which we stand, and we rejoice in our hope of sharing the glory of God.

Romans 5:2 RSV

Perfect Timing

Carolyn, a preacher's wife, had just found evidence that her daughter was involved in potentially deadly activities. Because of her position, however, Carolyn felt that to tell anyone this family secret might expose her husband and his ministry to ridicule or shame. To keep the secret was painful—she needed a friend. In near desperation, she cried out to God, "I've got to talk to *someone!* Can't You send me somebody I can trust?"

Almost before she had finished praying, the doorbell rang. When she opened the door, there stood another preacher's wife. She was new to the city and had come to make her acquaintance. Almost immediately the women developed a rapport as they discussed their lives, their many moves, and the difficulties of raising children.

Carolyn discovered her newfound friend had also gone through the struggle of raising a rebellious teenager. She poured out her problem to her new friend, who offered, "Would you mind if I prayed for you before I go?" Within minutes, Carolyn felt peace and hope fill her heart. She realized God had sent her help the very *minute* she needed it.

Hope in God is never misplaced. He always comes through. Even before we pray, an answer is on the way.

Hope

Praise be to the God and Father or our Lord Jesus Christ! In his great mercy he has given us new birth into a living hope through the resurrection of Jesus Christ from the dead, and into an inheritance that can never perish, spoil or fade— kept in heaven for you.

1 Peter 1:3-4

Lord, you alone are my hope; I've trusted you from childhood.

Psalm 71:5 TLB

May those who fear you rejoice when they see me, for I have put my hope in your word.

Psalm 119:74

Be of good courage, and he shall strengthen your heart, all ye that hope in the LORD.

Psalm 31:24 KJV

Stargazing

During the darkest days of the Civil War, the hopes of the Union nearly died. When certain goals seemed unreachable, the leaders of the Union turned to President Abraham Lincoln for solace, guidance, and hope. Once, when a delegation called at the White House and detailed a long list of crises facing the nation, Lincoln told this story:

> Years ago a young friend and I were out one night when a shower of meteors fell from the clear November sky. The young man was frightened, but I told him to look up in the sky past the shooting stars to the fixed stars beyond, shining serene in the firmament, and I said, "Let us not mind the meteors, but let us keep our eyes on the stars."

When times are troubled or life seems to be changing too much, keep your inner eyes of faith and hope on those things which you know to be lasting and sure. Don't limit your gaze to what you know or who you know, but focus on Whom you know. A relationship with God alone is the supreme goal. He is the source of all hope. He never changes. He will never be removed from His place as the King of Glory.

Integrity

I know, my God, that you test men to see if they are good; for you enjoy good men. I have done all this with good motives, and I have watched your people offer their gifts willingly and joyously.

1 Chronicles 29:17 TLB

May integrity and uprightness preserve me, for I wait for thee.

Psalm 25:21 RSV

He who walks in integrity walks securely, but he who perverts his ways will be found out.

Proverbs 10:9 RSV

The integrity of the upright guides them, but the crookedness of the treacherous destroys them.

Proverbs 11:3 RSV

The Best Pursuit

In 1947 Dr. Chandrasekhar was asked to teach an advanced seminar in astrophysics at the University of Chicago. At the time, he was living in Wisconsin, doing research at the Yerkes astronomical observatory. He faced a one-hundred mile commute twice a week in the dead of winter to teach the class, but he nonetheless agreed enthusiastically.

However, registration for the advanced seminar was far below expectations. In fact, only two students signed up for the class. Other faculty members expected Dr. Chandrasekhar to cancel the course, so as not to waste his valuable time. He determined, however, to continue with the course and give his very best to the two students registered.

Those students, Chen Ning Yang and Tsung-Dao Lee, made his efforts worthwhile. Ten years later, in 1957, they both won the Nobel prize for physics. In 1983, Dr. Chandrasekhar won that same award.

Ends and means are not meant to exist in conflict. Good means to good ends are what God challenges us to find and to do, regardless of the personal cost, the effort required, or the lack of resulting public acclaim. The best pursuit of the best ideals—that's what it means to have integrity.

Integrity

Till I die, I will not deny my integrity.
Job 27:5

And as for you, if you will walk before me, as
David your father walked, with integrity of heart
and uprightness, doing according to all that I have
commanded you and keeping my statutes and my
ordinances, then I will establish your royal throne
over Israel for ever, as I promised.
1 Kings 9:4-5 RSV

When the storm has swept by, the wicked are
gone, but the righteous stand firm forever.
Proverbs 10:25

By standing firm you will gain life.
Luke 21:19

The Hallmark of Integrity

Dwight L. Moody's father died when Dwight was only four. With nine mouths to feed and no income, the widow Moody was dogged by creditors. In response to the situation, the eldest son ran away from home. Few would have criticized Mrs. Moody for seeking assistance or letting others help raise her children. However, she was determined to keep her family together.

On a nightly basis, Mrs. Moody placed a light in the window, certain her son would return home. Dwight wrote of those days, "When the wind was very high and the house would tremble at every gust, the voice of my mother was raised in prayer." In time, her prayers were answered. Moody recalls that no one recognized his older brother when he came to the door, a great beard flowed down his chest. It was only as the tears began to soak his beard that Mrs. Moody recognized her son and invited him in. He said, "No, Mother, I will not come in until I hear first that you have forgiven me." She was only too willing to forgive, of course, and threw her arms around her son in a warm embrace.

Mrs. Moody didn't change just because her circumstances did. That is the hallmark of integrity.

Jealousy

For where you have envy and selfish ambition, there you find disorder and every evil practice.
James 3:16

Be still before the LORD and wait patiently for him; do not fret when men succeed in their ways, when they carry out their wicked schemes.
Psalm 37:7

If we live by the Spirit, let us also walk by the Spirit. Let us have no self-conceit, no provoking of one another, no envy of one another.
Galatians 5:25-26 RSV

You shall not covet your neighbor's house. You shall not covet your neighbor's wife, or his manservant or maidservant, his ox or donkey, or anything that belongs to your neighbor.
Exodus 20:17

Different, but the Same

At the height of the segregation storm in the United States, a six-year-old girl headed out for her first day of school. Her elementary school was one that had been integrated recently, and the community was still full of tension. After school her mother met her anxiously at the door, eager to hear how the day had gone. "Did everything go alright, honey?" she asked.

"Oh, Mother! You know what?" the little girl said eagerly, "A little black girl sat next to me."

With growing apprehension the mother asked, "And what happened?"

The little girl replied, "We were both so scared about our first day at school that we held hands all day."

Often, jealousy and hate are born out of a lack of information—we simply don't know a person or an individual member of a group. Once we discover the many things that we share in common with another person—including our fears, our hopes, our concerns, our desires—our differences simply enhance our relationships.

When we allow one another our unique differences, jealousy fades and love grows.

Jealousy

For the wicked boasteth of his heart's desire, and blesseth the covetous, whom the LORD abhorreth.

Psalm 10:3 KJV

Wrath is cruel, anger is overwhelming; but who can stand before jealousy?

Proverbs 27:4 RSV

Then I observed that the basic motive for success is the driving force of envy and jealousy! But this, too, is foolishness, chasing the wind.

Ecclesiastes 4:4 TLB

But if you harbor bitter envy and selfish ambition in your hearts, do not boast about it or deny the truth.

James 3:14

How to Live

Few people have undergone the trials and tribulations of Alexander Solzhenitsyn, who suffered decades of horrendous hardship as a political exile in the Siberian prison system known as the "gulag." We can learn from Solzhenitsyn not only because he is a survivor, but because he has been in a situation that few of us have ever known—an existence of near total deprivation. He has not only lived without luxuries, but without necessities.

He writes as few can in *The Prison Chronicle:*

Don't be afraid of misfortune and do not yearn after happiness. It is, after all, all the same. The bitter doesn't last forever, and the sweet never fills the cup to overflowing. It is enough if you don't freeze in the cold and if hunger and thirst don't claw at your sides. If your back isn't broken, if your feet can walk, if both arms work, if both eyes can see, and if both ears can hear, then whom should you envy? And why? Our envy and jealousy devour us most of all. Rub your eyes and purify your heart and prize above all else in the world those who love you and wish you well.

Joy

For you shall go out in joy, and be led forth in peace; the mountains and the hills before you shall break forth into singing, and all the trees of the field shall clap their hands.

Isaiah 55:12 RSV

And the ransomed of the LORD shall return, and come to Zion with singing; everlasting joy shall be upon their heads; they shall obtain joy and gladness, and sorrow and sighing shall flee away.

Isaiah 51:11 RSV

Yes, the gladness you have given me is far greater than their joys at harvest time as they gaze at their bountiful crops.

Psalm 4:7 TLB

Then he said to them, "Go your way, eat the fat and drink sweet wine and send portions to him for whom nothing is prepared; for this day is holy to our LORD; and do not be grieved, for the joy of the LORD is your strength."

Nehemiah 8:10 RSV

The Joy of Little Cranberry Island

Joy Sprague knows how to brighten the days of her customers. As the postmaster for Little Cranberry Island, Maine, she actually has customers competing to get their pictures on her post-office wall. Every twenty-fifth customer to use the U.S. Postal Service's Express Mail has a "mug shot" taken which is hung on the wall. They also receive a plate of Joy's home-baked cream puffs!

That's not all Joy does to make Little Cranberry, population 90, a friendlier place. She operates a mail-order stamp business that is so popular her tiny post office ranks fourth in sales out of 450 outlets in Maine. Why? Most of Joy's customers are summer visitors who want to stay up to date with the news of the island. Along with each order, Joy sends a snapshot of an island scene and a handwritten note about island events.

One of the residents has remarked, "She invents ways to bring pleasure to others." Joy has received praise from the U.S. Postmaster General and has the warm affection not only of the local residents, but friends across America who delight in corresponding with her.

Why not ask the Lord to give you creative ideas which will bring joy to someone's life today?

Joy

No wonder we are happy in the Lord! For we are trusting him. We trust his holy name.

Psalm 33:21 TLB

I will greatly rejoice in the LORD, my soul shall exult in my God; for he has clothed me with the garments of salvation, he has covered me with the robe of righteousness, as a bridegroom decks himself with a garland, and as a bride adorns herself with her jewels.

Isaiah 61:10 RSV

May those who sow in tears reap with shouts of joy! He that goes forth weeping, bearing the seed for sowing, shall come home with shouts of joy, bringing his sheaves with him.

Psalm 126:5-6 RSV

So you have sorrow now, but I will see you again and your hearts will rejoice, and no one will take your joy from you.

John 16:22 RSV

Cries of Hallelujah

Handel's masterpiece, *The Messiah*, has inspired millions through the centuries. Few know, however, that George Frederick Handel composed *The Messiah* in approximately three weeks. The music literally came to him in a flurry of notes and motifs. He composed feverishly, as if driven by the unseen Composer. It is also little known that Handel composed the work while his eyesight was failing or that he was facing the threat of debtor's prison because of outstanding bills. Most people find it difficult to create under stress, especially when physical or financial problems are the root of that stress. And yet, Handel did.

He credits the completion of the work to one thing: joy. He was quoted as saying that he felt as if his heart would burst with joy at what he was hearing in his mind and heart. It was joy that compelled him to write, forced him to create, and ultimately found expression in the "Hallelujah Chorus."

Handel lived to see his oratorio become a cherished tradition. He was especially pleased to see it performed to raise money for benevolent causes.

When joy is present, Jesus Christ is expressed.

Justice

The Almighty is beyond our reach and exalted in power; in his justice and great righteousness, he does not oppress.

Job 37:23

Arise, O LORD, in thy anger, lift thyself up against the fury of my enemies; awake, O my God; thou hast appointed a judgment.

Psalm 7:6 RSV

But let him who glories glory in this, that he understands and knows me, that I am the LORD who practice steadfast love, justice, and righteousness in the earth; for in these things I delight.

Jeremiah 9:24 RSV

Follow justice and justice alone, so that you may live and possess the land the LORD your God is giving you.

Deuteronomy 16:20

Endangered Justice

To crack the lily-white system of higher education in Georgia in the 1960s, black leaders decided they needed to find two "squeaky-clean students" who couldn't be challenged on moral, intellectual, or educational grounds. In a discussion about who might be chosen, Alfred Holmes immediately volunteered his son, Hamilton, the top black male senior in the city. Charlayne Hunter-Gault also stepped forward and expressed an interest in applying to the university. Georgia delayed admitting both boys on grounds it had no room in its dormitories, and the matter eventually ended up in federal court. Judge Bootle ordered the university to admit the two, who were qualified in every respect; and thus, segregation ended at the university level in that state, and soon, the nation.

Attorney General Robert Kennedy declared in a speech not long after: "We know that it is the law which enables men to live together, that creates order out of chaos. . . . And we know that if one man's rights are denied, the rights of all are endangered."

Justice may be universal, but it always begins at the individual level. Who might you treat more "justly" today?

Justice

Help him to give justice to your people, even to the poor.

Psalm 72:2 TLB

He does not crush the weak, Or quench the smallest hope; He will end all conflict with his final victory, And his name shall be the hope Of all the world.

Matthew 12:20-21 TLB

God presented him as a sacrifice of atonement, through faith in his blood. He did this to demonstrate his justice, because in his forbearance he had left the sins committed beforehand unpunished—he did it to demonstrate his justice at the present time, so as to be just and the one who justifies those who have faith in Jesus.

Romans 3:25-26

Learn to do well; seek judgment, relieve the oppressed, judge the fatherless, plead for the widow.

Isaiah 1:17 KJV

True Justice

One of New York City's most popular mayors was Fiorello LaGuardia. One time he read the funny papers over the radio, with all the appropriate inflections, because a strike had kept the Sunday newspapers off the stands. Others remember his outbursts against the "bums" who exploited the poor.

One time, the mayor chose to preside in a night court. An old woman was brought before him on that bitterly cold night. The charge was stealing a loaf of bread. She explained that her family was starving. LaGuardia replied, "I've got to punish you. The law makes no exception. I must fine you ten dollars." At that, he reached into his own pocket and pulled out a ten-dollar bill. "Well," he said, "here's the ten dollars to pay your fine, which I now remit." He then tossed the ten-dollar bill into his own hat and declared, "I'm going to fine everybody in this courtroom fifty cents for living in a town where a person has to steal bread in order to eat. Mr. Bailiff, collect the fines and give them to this defendant."

After the hat was passed, the incredulous old woman left the courtroom with a new light in her eyes and $47.50 in her pocket to buy groceries!

Loneliness

Behold, I am with you and will keep you wherever you go, and will bring you back to this land; for I will not leave you until I have done that of which I have spoken to you.

Genesis 28:15 RSV

God sets the lonely in families, he leads forth the prisoners with singing.

Psalm 68:6

All those who know your mercy, Lord, will count on you for help. For you have never yet forsaken those who trust in you.

Psalm 9:10 TLB

I will never, never fail you nor forsake you.

Hebrews 13:5 TLB

Who's Holding You Up?

Many years ago, a young woman who felt called into the ministry was accepted into seminary. There were only two other women enrolled there, and her very presence seemed to make her male classmates uncomfortable. She felt isolated, yet on display. To make matters worse, many of her professors were doing their best to destroy her faith rather than build it up. Even her private devotions seemed dry and lonely.

At Christmas break she sought her father's counsel. "How can I be strong in my resolve and straight in my theology with all that I face there?"

Her father took a pencil from his pocket and laid it on the palm of his hand. "Can that pencil stand upright by itself?" he asked her.

"No," she replied. Then her father grasped the pencil in his hand and held it in an upright position. "Ah," she said, "but you are holding it now."

"Daughter," he replied, "your life is like this pencil. But Jesus Christ is the one who can hold you."

Whatever difficulties you may confront today, remember it is God who holds you in His hands. His strength holds you up and enables you to face anything that comes your way.

Loneliness

The eternal God is thy refuge, and underneath
are the everlasting arms: and he shall thrust out
the enemy from before thee; and shall say,
Destroy them.

Deuteronomy 33:27 KJV

Hence we can confidently say, "The Lord is my
helper, I will not be afraid; what can man do
to me?"

Hebrews 13:6 RSV

Who shall separate us from the love of Christ?
Shall trouble or hardship or persecution or famine
or nakedness or danger or sword? No, in all these
things we are more than conquerors through him
who loved us. For I am convinced that neither
death nor life, neither angels nor demons, neither
the present nor the future, nor any powers,
neither height nor depth, nor anything else in all
creation, will be able to separate us from the love
of God that is in Christ Jesus our Lord.

Romans 8:35, 37-39

Be still, and know that I am God; I will be exalted
among the nations, I will be exalted in the earth.

Psalm 46:10

Being Rooted

The next time you visit a very dense forest, try to imagine what is taking place under your feet. Scientists now know when the roots of trees come into contact with one another, a substance is released which encourages the growth of a particular kind of fungus. This fungus helps link roots of different trees—even those of dissimilar species. If one tree has access to water, another to nutrients, and a third to sunlight, the fungus enables the transfer of these items to trees that may be in need. Thus, the trees have the means of sharing with one another to preserve them all.

Our culture today applauds individualism. However, it tends to isolate people from one another and cut them off from the mainstream of life. With more and more people working at home or in walled offices and with schedules crammed tighter than ever with work and activities, feelings of loneliness are more likely to increase than decrease. Don't allow isolation to overcome you!

Reach out to others. Begin to give where you can. Learn to receive when others give to you. Build a network of friends, not just colleagues. And above all, root yourself into a group that nourishes and builds you up spiritually—your church.

Love

And now these three remain: faith, hope and love.
But the greatest of these is love.

1 Corinthians 13:13

Work instead at what is right and good, learning
to trust him and love others, and to be patient
and gentle.

1 Timothy 6:11 TLB

Above all, love each other deeply, because love
covers over a multitude of sins.

1 Peter 4:8

And above all these put on love, which binds
everything together in perfect harmony.

Colossians 3:14 RSV

An Umbrella of Love

In Bible times, apartment-style homes were built atop city walls. Part of the roof extended beyond the walls to protect them from rain and sun. The word for this overhang is translated, "forbear," in English. It literally means to "outroof." This is the way God commands us to love—to forbear one another in love, or to "outroof" one another—to protect those you love with your love, rather than expose them and their faults.

This does not mean we are to be blind to error or live in a state of denial about wrongs committed around us or to us. It simply means we choose to love so much that our love overshadows the hurt those wrongs may have done. We recognize that we can never know the "whole story" about another person or event. We can only know so much about their motives or what's in their heart. However, we can choose not to focus on those things we don't understand but focus instead on what we can do: love.

As one old minister once told his country congregation, "God invites us to be His partner in everything but judging people." "Outroof" your family and friends with your love today.

Love

For God so loved the world that he gave his only Son, that whoever believes in him should not perish but have eternal life.

John 3:16 RSV

And he will love thee, and bless thee, and multiply thee.

Deuteronomy 7:13 KJV

The LORD sets prisoners free, the LORD gives sight to the blind, the LORD lifts up those who are bowed down, the LORD loves the righteous.

Psalm 146:7-8

The LORD your God is with you, he is mighty to save. He will take great delight in you, he will quiet you with his love, he will rejoice over you with singing.

Zephaniah 3:17

Adopted to Belong

A Sunday school superintendent was registering two new boys in Sunday school. She asked their ages and birthdays so she could place them in the appropriate classes. The bolder of the two replied, "We're both seven. My birthday is April 8 and my brother's birthday is April 20." The superintendent replied, "But that's not possible, boys." The quieter brother spoke up. "No, it's true. One of us is adopted."

"Oh?" asked the superintendent. "Which one?" The two brothers looked at each other and smiled. The bolder one said, "We asked Dad that same question awhile ago, but he just looked at us and said he loved us both equally, and he couldn't remember anymore which one of us was adopted."

What a wonderful analogy of God's love! The Apostle Paul wrote to the Romans: "Now if we are [God's] children, then we are heirs—heirs of God and co-heirs with Christ" (Romans 8:17). In essence, as adopted sons and daughters of God, we fully share in the inheritance of His only begotten Son, Jesus. Our Heavenly Father has adopted us and loves us just as much as His beloved Son.

Marriage

And the LORD God said, It is not good that the man should be alone; I will make him an help meet for him.

Genesis 2:18 KJV

Therefore what God has joined together, let man not separate.

Matthew 19:6

He who finds a wife finds what is good and receives favor from the LORD.

Proverbs 18:22

But I want you to understand that the head of every man is Christ, the head of a woman is her husband, and the head of Christ is God.

1 Corinthians 11:3 RSV

Promises

In Thornton Wilder's play *The Skin of Our Teeth*, the character Mrs. Antrobus says to her husband, "I didn't marry you because you were perfect. . . . I married you because you gave me a promise."

She then takes off her ring and looks at it, saying, "That promise made up for your faults and the promise I gave you made up for mine. Two imperfect people got married, and it was the promise that made the marriage."

In every marriage, no matter how well the two people know one another, great mysteries remain! Very often, each person comes to the marriage

- not fully knowing himself or herself,
- not fully knowing about life, and
- not fully knowing about his or her spouse.

What is unknown is far greater than what is known!

Becoming a faithful, loving spouse not only takes courage and faith, but patience and a desire to keep learning and growing. Better than asking, "What kind of spouse do I desire to have?" is the question, "What kind of spouse do I aspire to be?"

Marriage

Therefore a man leaves his father and his mother and cleaves to his wife, and they become one flesh.

Genesis 2:24 RSV

You wives, submit yourselves to your husbands, for that is what the Lord has planned for you. And you husbands must be loving and kind to your wives and not bitter against them, nor harsh.

Colossians 3:18-19 TLB

You husbands must be careful of your wives, being thoughtful of their needs and honoring them. . . . Remember that you and your wife are partners in receiving God's blessings.

1 Peter 3:7 TLB

For the husband is the head of the wife, even as Christ is the head of the church: And he is the saviour of the body.

Ephesians 5:23 KJV

Move It!

Newspaper columnist and minister George Crane tells of a wife who came to his office full of hatred toward her husband. Fully intending to divorce her husband, she said, "Before I divorce him, I want to hurt him as much as he has me."

Crane advised that she go home and act as if she really loved her husband. "Tell him how much he means to you," he said. "Praise him for every decent trait. Go out of your way to be as kind, considerate, and generous as possible. Spare no efforts to please him, to enjoy him. Make him believe you love him . . . then drop the bomb. . . . That will really hurt him."

The woman exclaimed, "Beautiful!" And she did as he had suggested with enthusiasm, acting as if she loved him. Two months later she returned to Crane, who asked, "Are you ready to go through with the divorce?"

"Divorce!" she said. "Never! I discovered I really do love him!"

Actions can change feelings. Motion can result in emotion. Love is established not so much by fervent promise as by often-repeated deeds.

Mercy

Let us therefore come boldly unto the throne of grace, that we may obtain mercy, and find grace to help in time of need.

Hebrews 4:16 KJV

I will make all my goodness pass before thee, and I will proclaim the name of the LORD before thee; and will be gracious to whom I will be gracious, and will show mercy on whom I will show mercy.

Exodus 33:19 KJV

Give knowledge of salvation to his people in the forgiveness of their sins, through the tender mercy of our God.

Luke 1:77-78 RSV

The LORD is gracious, and full of compassion; slow to anger, and of great mercy. The LORD is good to all: and his tender mercies are over all his works.

Psalm 145:8-9 KJV

How Big a Person?

When William Gladstone was Chancellor of the Exchequer, he once requested that the Treasury send him certain statistics upon which he might base his budget proposals. The statistician made a mistake. But Gladstone was so certain of this man's concern for accuracy that he didn't take the time to verify the figures. As a result, he went before the House of Commons and made a speech based upon the incorrect figures. His speech was no sooner published than the inaccuracies were exposed, and Gladstone became the brunt of public ridicule.

The Chancellor sent for the statistician who had given him the erroneous information. The man arrived full of fear and shame, certain he was going to be let go. Instead, Gladstone said, "I know how much you must be disturbed over what has happened, and I have sent for you to put you at your ease. For a long time you have been engaged in handling the intricacies of the national accounts, and this is the first mistake that you have made. I want to congratulate you, and express to you my keen appreciation."

It takes a big person to extend mercy, a big person to listen rather than talk, a big person to think before jumping into action.

Mercy

Who is a God like you, who pardons sin and forgives the transgression of the remnant of his inheritance? You do not stay angry forever but delight to show mercy.

Micah 7:18

Foreigners will come and build your cities. Presidents and kings will send you aid. For though I destroyed you in my anger, I will have mercy on you through my grace.

Isaiah 60:10 TLB

Yet the Lord still waits for you to come to him, so he can show you his love; he will conquer you to bless you, just as he said. For the Lord is faithful to his promises. Blessed are all those who wait for him to help them.

Isaiah 30:18 TLB

But the lovingkindness of the Lord is from everlasting to everlasting, to those who reverence him; his salvation is to children's children of those who are faithful to his covenant and remember to obey him!

Psalm 103:17-18 TLB

In Need of Mercy

According to a traditional Hebrew legend, Abraham was sitting by his tent one evening when he saw an old man walking toward him. He could tell long before the man arrived that he was weary from age and travel. Abraham rushed out to greet him, and then invited him into his tent. He washed the old man's feet and gave him something to drink and eat.

The old man immediately began eating without saying a prayer. Abraham asked him, "Don't you worship God?" The old traveler replied, "I worship fire only and reverence no other god." Upon hearing this, Abraham grabbed the old man by the shoulders and threw him out of his tent.

The old man walked off into the night and after he had gone, God called to His friend Abraham and asked where the stranger was. Abraham replied, "I forced him out of my tent because he did not worship You." The Lord responded, "I have suffered him these eighty years although he dishonors Me. Could you not endure him one night?"

Do you know someone who needs to experience your mercy as a tangible expression of the mercy God is extending to him or her? Don't turn them away; take them in.

Obedience

For whosoever shall do the will of my Father which is in heaven, the same as my brother, and sister, and mother.

Matthew 12:50 KJV

Don't you know that when you offer yourselves to someone to obey him as slaves, you are slaves to the one whom you obey—whether you are slaves to sin, which leads to death, or to obedience, which leads to righteousness?

Romans 6:16

And Samuel said, Hath the LORD as great delight in burnt offerings and sacrifices, as in obeying the voice of the LORD? Behold, to obey is better than sacrifice, and to hearken than the fat of rams.

1 Samuel 15:22 KJV

If they obey and serve him, they will spend the rest of their days in prosperity and their years in contentment.

Job 36:11

Obedient Choices

In the eleventh century, King Henry III of Bavaria became tired of his responsibilities as king, the pressures of international politics, and the mundane worldliness of court life. He made an application to Prior Richard at a local monastery to be accepted as a contemplative, to spend the rest of his life in prayer and meditation there.

Prior Richard responded, "Your Majesty, do you understand that the pledge here is one of obedience? That will be hard for you since you have been a king."

"I understand," Henry said. "The rest of my life I will be obedient to you, as Christ leads you."

Prior Richard responded, "Then I will tell you what to do. Go back to your throne and serve faithfully in the place where God has put you."

After King Henry died, this statement was written in his honor: "The king learned to rule by being obedient."

Each of us ultimately obeys either the righteous commandments of our Heavenly Father or the "rule of lawlessness." We must willingly choose to put ourselves under authority, including the authority of God. To fail to do so is to have no law other than our own whim, an unreliable source at its best!

Obedience

He who has my commandments and keeps them,
he it is who loves me; and he who loves me will
be loved by my Father, and I will love him and
manifest myself to him.

John 14:21 RSV

Because of your obedience, the Lord your God
will keep his part of the contract which, in his
tender love, he made with your fathers.

Deuteronomy 7:12 TLB

When you obey me you are living in my love, just
as I obey my Father and live in his love.

John 15:10 TLB

But, dearly loved friends, if our consciences are
clear, we can come to the Lord with perfect
assurance and trust, and get whatever we ask for
because we are obeying him and doing the things
that please him.

1 John 3:21-22 TLB

Coming Clean

Professional stock-car racer Darrell Waltrip was once proud of his image as "the guy folks loved to hate." Then things began to change. After miraculously surviving a crash in the Daytona 500, he began going to church with his wife, Stevie. They began trying to have a family, but suffered four miscarriages.

One day their pastor came to visit. He asked, "Your car is sponsored by a beer company. Is that the image you want?" Darrell had never thought about it. He had always loved watching kids admire his car, but the more he thought about it, he discovered that he did care about his image. He thought, *If our prayers were answered for a child, what kind of dad would I be?*

He didn't know what to do to convince his car's owner to change sponsors, but amazingly, an opportunity opened for him to sign with a new racing team sponsored by a laundry detergent company! He switched teams. Two years later, daughter Jessica was born, and a few years later, daughter Sarah. In 1989, he won the Daytona.

Obedience to God and His Word opens the doors for God to rain down blessings on our lives.

Patience

You need to keep on patiently doing God's will if you want him to do for you all that he has promised.

Hebrews 10:36 TLB

Dear brothers, is your life full of difficulties and temptations? Then be happy, for when the way is rough, your patience has a chance to grow. So let it grow, and don't try to squirm out of your problems. For when your patience is finally in full bloom, then you will be ready for anything, strong in character, full and complete.

James 1:2-4 TLB

For ye have need of patience, that, after ye have done the will of God, ye might receive the promise.

Hebrews 10:36 KJV

Finishing is better than starting! Patience is better than pride! Don't be quick-tempered—that is being a fool.

Ecclesiastes 7:8-9 TLB

Impatience

"Have you, perchance, found a diamond pendant? I feel certain I lost it last night in your theater," a woman phoned to ask the theater manager.

"Not that I know, madam," the manager said, "but let me ask some of my employees. Please hold the line for a minute while I make inquiry. If it hasn't been found, we certainly will make a diligent search for it."

Returning to the phone a few minutes later, the manager said, "I have good news for you! The diamond pendant has been found!"

There was no reply to his news however. "Hello! Hello!" he called into the phone, and then he heard the dial tone. The woman who made the inquiry about the lost diamond pendant had failed to wait for his answer. She had not given her name, and attempts to trace her call were unsuccessful. The pendant was eventually sold to raise money for the theater.

We are often like this woman when we make our requests to God. We fail to wait on the Lord, to hear His reply. Instead, we rush ahead impatiently, having no idea He has a great blessing to give us if only we'd slow down long enough to receive it!

Patience

And so, as those who have been chosen of God, holy and beloved, put on a heart of compassion, kindness, humility, gentleness and patience; bearing with one another, and forgiving each other, whoever has a complaint against anyone; just as the Lord forgave you, so also should you.

Colossians 3:12-13 NAS

Be humble and gentle. Be patient with each other, making allowance for each other's faults because of your love.

Ephesians 4:2 TLB

You will be anxious to follow the example of those who receive all that God has promised them because of their strong faith and patience.

Hebrews 6:12 TLB

You too be patient; strengthen your hearts, for the coming of the Lord is at hand.

James 5:8 NAS

Genius

We often think of great artists and musicians as having "bursts" of genius. More often, they are models of painstaking patience. Their greatest works tend to have been accomplished over long periods, and often through extreme hardship.

Beethoven is said to have rewritten each bar of his music at least a dozen times.

Josef Haydn produced more than 800 musical compositions before writing "The Creation," the oratorio for which he is most famous.

Michelangelo's "Last Judgment" is considered one of the twelve master paintings of the ages. It took him eight years to complete. He produced more than 2,000 sketches and renderings in the process.

Leonardo da Vinci worked on "The Last Supper" for ten years, often working so diligently that he forgot to eat.

When he was quite elderly, the pianist Ignace Paderewski was asked by an admirer, "Is it true that you still practice every day?" He replied, "Yes, at least six hours a day." The admirer said in awe, "You must have a world of patience." Paderewski said, "I have no more patience than the next fellow. I just use mine."

Use your patience today, then the next day and the next. Your masterpiece is waiting to be completed.

Persecution

Remember the words I spoke to you: "No servant is greater than his master." If they persecuted me, they will persecute you also.

John 15:20

Blessed are those who have been persecuted for the sake of righteousness, for theirs is the kingdom of heaven. Blessed are you when men cast insults at you, and persecute you, and say all kinds of evil against you falsely, on account of Me.

Matthew 5:10-11 NAS

But of course you know that such troubles are a part of God's plan for us Christians. Even while we were still with you we warned you ahead of time that suffering would soon come—and it did.

1 Thessalonians 3:3-4 TLB

In fact, everyone who wants to live a godly life in Christ Jesus will be persecuted.

2 Timothy 3:12

A Greater Weapon

Joseph Ton ran away from his native Romania to study theology at Oxford. As he was preparing to return to his homeland after graduation, he shared his plans with several students. They candidly pointed out to him that he would probably be arrested at the border. One asked, "If you're arrested, what hope do you have of being a preacher?"

Ton asked God about this and was reminded of Matthew 10:16, "I send you out as sheep in the midst of wolves" (NKJV). He thought, *What chance does a sheep have of surviving, let alone converting, the wolves? Yet Jesus sent them out and expected them not only to survive, but to fulfill His mission.*

He returned to his country and preached until the day he was arrested. As he was being interrogated by officials, Joseph said: "Your supreme weapon is killing, mine is dying. My sermons are all over the country on tapes now. If you kill me, then whoever listens to them will say, 'This must be true. This man sealed his words with his blood.' The tapes will speak ten times louder than before, so go on and kill me. I win the supreme victory." The officer sent him home!

Persecution

I say: Love your enemies! Pray for those who persecute you! In that way you will be acting as true sons of your Father in heaven.

Matthew 5:44-45 TLB

If someone mistreats you because you are a Christian, don't curse him; pray that God will bless him.

Romans 12:14 TLB

Listen, all of you. Love your enemies. Do good to those who hate you. Pray for the happiness of those who curse you; implore God's blessing on those who hurt you.

Luke 6:27-28 TLB

If your enemy is hungry, give him food to eat; and if he is thirsty, give him water to drink; for you will heap burning coals on his head, and the Lord will reward you.

Proverbs 25:21-22 NAS

Equal and Opposite

The bathysphere is an amazing invention. Operating like a miniature submarine, bathyspheres have been used to explore the ocean in places so deep the water pressure would crush a conventional submarine as easily as if it were an aluminum can. Bathyspheres compensate for the intense water pressure with plates of steel several inches thick. The steel withstands the water pressure, but it also makes a bathysphere very heavy and hard to maneuver. The inside is tiny and cramped, allowing for only one or two people to survey the ocean floor through a tiny plate-glass window.

Amazingly, divers find fish and other sea creatures at every depth of the ocean! Some of these creatures are quite small and have normal-looking skin. No heavy metal for them! They swim freely, remaining flexible and supple in the inky waters.

How is it that fish can live at these depths without being crushed? They compensate for the outside pressure with equal and opposite pressure from inside.

Spiritual fortitude works in the same way. The greater the persecution we experience, the greater the need for us to allow God's power to work within us to exert an equal and opposite pressure.

Perseverance

May the Lord direct your hearts into God's love and Christ's perseverance.

2 Thessalonians 3:5

[Love] always protects, always trusts, always hopes, always perseveres.

1 Corinthians 13:7

We also rejoice in our sufferings, because we know that suffering produces perseverance; perseverance, character; and character, hope. And hope does not disappoint us, because God has poured out his love into our hearts by the Holy Spirit, whom he has given us.

Romans 5:3-5

Because you know that the testing of your faith develops perseverance. Perseverance must finish its work so that you may be mature and complete, not lacking anything.

James 1:3-4

Pedal Faster!

Success in business is often closely associated with a person's courage and ability to recover from his or her most recent failure.

In 1928, a thirty-three-year-old man by the name of Paul Galvin, found himself staring at failure—again. He had failed in business twice at this point, his competitors having forced him to fold his latest venture in the storage battery business. Convinced, however, that he still had a marketable idea, Galvin attended the auction of his own business. With $750 he had managed to raise, he bought back the battery eliminator portion of the inventory. With it, he built a new company—one in which he succeeded. He eventually retired from his company, but not before it became a household name: Motorola. Upon his retirement, Galvin advised others: "Do not fear mistakes. You will know failure—continue to reach out."

A failure isn't truly a failure until you quit trying. If a venture begins to slow down, try speeding up your efforts. Consider the child who quits pedaling their bike. Eventually the bicycle wobbles to the point where the child falls off. The key to avoiding the crash? Faster peddling! The same holds true for many an enterprise. Don't give up; just pedal faster!

Perseverance

Supplement your faith with virtue, and virtue with knowledge, and knowledge with self-control, and self-control with steadfastness, and steadfastness with godliness, and godliness with brotherly affection, and brotherly affection with love. For if these things are yours and abound, they keep you from being ineffective or unfruitful in the knowledge of our Lord Jesus Christ.

2 Peter 1:5-8 RSV

You need to persevere so that when you have done the will of God, you will receive what he has promised.

Hebrews 10:36

Watch your life and doctrine closely. Preservere in them, because if you do, you will save both yourself and your hearers.

1 Timothy 4:16

But the seed on good soil stands for those with a noble and good heart, who hear the word, retain it, and by persevering produce a crop.

Luke 8:15

The Kid Who Couldn't Sit Still

Nelson Diebel, a hyperactive and delinquent child, was enrolled in The Peddie School. There he met swimming coach Chris Martin, who believed the more one practices, the better one performs. Within a month, he had Nelson swimming thirty to forty hours a week, even though Nelson could not sit still in a classroom for fifteen minutes. Martin saw potential in Nelson. He constantly put new goals in front of him, trying to get him to focus and turn his anger into strength. Nelson eventually qualified for the Junior Nationals, where his times qualified him for the Olympic trials.

However, Nelson broke both hands and arms in a diving accident, and doctors warned he probably would never regain his winning form. Martin said to him, "You're coming all the way back. . . . If you're not committed to that, we're going to stop right now." Nelson agreed and within weeks after his casts were off, he was swimming again. In 1992, he won Olympic gold. As he accepted his medal, he recalls thinking, *The kid who once couldn't sit still and who had no ambition . . . had learned to make a plan, pursue it, and achieve it.* He had persevered and come out a champion!

Priorities

Seek the LORD and his strength, seek his presence continually! Remember the wonderful works that he has done, the wonders he wrought, the judgments he uttered.

1 Chronicles 16:11-12 RSV

Let the word of Christ dwell in you richly in all wisdom; teaching and admonishing one another in psalms and hymns and spiritual songs, singing with grace in your hearts to the Lord. And whatsoever ye do in word or deed, do all in the name of the Lord Jesus, giving thanks to God and the Father by him.

Colossians 3:16-17 KJV

God, my God! How I search for you! How I thirst for you in this parched and weary land where there is no water. How I long to find you! At last I shall be fully satisfied; I will praise you with great joy.

Psalm 63:1, 5 TLB

What good will it be for a man if he gains the whole world, yet forfeits his soul?

Matthew 16:26

The Gift of Life

Once a nationally syndicated columnist and now an author, Anna Quindlen seems to have enjoyed success at everything she has attempted. However, in taking a fellow commentator to task after he made light of teenage problems, Anna was reminded of the two attempts she had made to end her own life at age sixteen. She writes, "I was really driven through my high school years. I always had to be perfect in every way, ranging from how I looked to how my grades were. It was too much pressure."

In the early 1970s, Anna's mother died from ovarian cancer. This tragedy cured Anna from any desire to commit suicide. Her attitude toward life changed. "I could never look at life as anything but a great gift. I realized I didn't have any business taking it for granted."

When we are faced with the realization that life is temporary, we can finally come to grips with what is important. When we face our own immortality, our priorities quickly come into focus.

Consider your life as God's gift to you. Every moment is precious, so cherish them all. In doing so, you'll find purpose and meaning for each day.

Priorities

If any man will come after me, let him deny himself, and take up his cross daily, and follow me. For whosoever will save his life shall lose it: but whosoever will lose his life for my sake, the same shall save it. For what is a man advantaged, if he gain the whole world, and lose himself, or be cast away?

Luke 9:23-25 KJV

Speak to one another with psalms, hymns and spiritual songs. Sing and make music in your heart to the Lord, always giving thanks to God the Father for everything, in the name of our Lord Jesus Christ.

Ephesians 5:19-20

By him therefore let us offer the sacrifice of praise to God continually, that is, the fruit of our lips giving thanks to his name.

Hebrews 13:15 KJV

I appeal to you therefore, brethren, by the mercies of God, to present your bodies as a living sacrifice, holy and acceptable to God, which is your spiritual worship.

Romans 12:1 RSV

To Please the Master

A young man once studied violin under a world-renowned violinist. He worked hard for several years perfecting his talent, and the day finally came when he was called upon to give his first major public recital in the large city where both he and his teacher lived. Following each selection, which he performed with great skill and passion, the performer seemed uneasy about the great applause he received. Even though he knew those in the audience were musically astute and not likely to give such applause to a less than superior performance, the young man acted almost as if he couldn't hear the appreciation that was being showered upon him.

At the close of the last number, the applause was thunderous and numerous "Bravos" were shouted. The talented young violinist, however, had his eyes glued on only one spot. Finally, when an elderly man in the first row of the balcony smiled and nodded to him in approval, the young man relaxed and beamed with both relief and joy. His teacher had praised his work! The applause of thousands meant nothing until he had first won the approval of the master. His top priority was to please his teacher.

Who are you most trying to please today?

Protection

If you make the Most High your dwelling—even the LORD, who is my refuge—then no harm will befall you, no disaster will come near your tent. For he will command his angels concerning you to guard you in all your ways; they will lift you up in their hands, so that you will not strike your foot against a stone.

Psalm 91:9-12

No weapon forged against you will prevail, and you will refute every tongue that accuses you. This is the heritage of the servants of the LORD, and this is their vindication from me.

Isaiah 54:17

In peace I will both lie down and sleep; for thou alone, O LORD, makest me dwell in safety.

Psalm 4:8 RSV

The LORD will keep you from all harm—he will watch over your life; the LORD will watch over your coming and going both now and forevermore.

Psalm 121:7-8

A Real Traffic-stopper

While driving along the freeway, the adults in the front seat of a car were talking when suddenly, they heard the horrifying sound of a car door opening, the whistle of wind, and a sickening thud. They quickly turned and saw that the three-year-old child riding in the back seat had fallen out of the car and was tumbling along the freeway. The driver screeched to a stop, and then raced back toward her child. To her surprise, she found that all the traffic had stopped just a few feet away from her child. Her daughter had not been hit.

A truck driver drove the girl to a nearby hospital. The doctors there rushed her into the emergency room, and soon came back with the good news: other than a few scrapes and bruises, the girl was fine; no broken bones, no apparent internal damage.

As the mother rushed to her child, the little girl opened her eyes and said, "Mommy, you know I wasn't afraid. While I was lying on the road waiting for you to get back to me, I looked up and right there I saw Jesus holding back the traffic with His arms out."

God truly watches over us with loving care.

Protection

But now, this is what the LORD says—he who created you, O Jacob, he who formed you, O Israel: "Fear not, for I have redeemed you; I have summoned you by name; you are mine. When you pass through the waters, I will be with you; and when you pass through the rivers, they will not sweep over you. When you walk through the fire, you will not be burned; the flames will not set you ablaze.

Isaiah 43:1-2

The angel of the LORD encamps around those who fear him, and he delivers them. Taste and see that the LORD is good; blessed is the man who takes refuge in him.

Psalm 34:7-8

The Lord is a strong fortress. The godly run to him and are safe.

Proverbs 18:10 TLB

He does not fear bad news, nor live in dread of what may happen. For he is settled in his mind that Jehovah will take care of him.

Psalm 112:7 TLB

Shelter

Have you ever explored a tidal pool? Low tide is the perfect time to find a myriad of creatures that have temporarily washed ashore from the depths of the sea.

Children are often amazed that they can pick up these shelled creatures and stare at them eyeball to eyeball. The creatures rarely exhibit any form of overt fear, such as moving to attack or attempting to scurry away. The creatures simply withdraw into their shells, instinctively knowing they are safe as long as they remain in their nice, strong shelters.

Likewise, we are safe when we remain in Christ. We are protected from the hassles of life, the unknowns, the bites and stings of temptation. Those things will come against us, much like the fingers of a brave and curious child trying to invade the sea creature's shell, but they have no power to harm us when we retreat into the shelter of Christ.

The Lord commanded us to learn to abide in Him and to remain steadfast in our faith. He tells us to trust in Him absolutely, and to shelter ourselves under His strong wings and in the cleft of His rock-like presence. He delights when we retreat into His arms for comfort and tender expressions of love.

Rejection

How great is the love the Father has lavished on us, that we should be called children of God! And that is what we are! The reason the world does not know us is that it did not know him. Dear friends, now we are children of God, and what we will be has not yet been made known.

1 John 3:1-2

A man of many companions may come to ruin, but there is a friend who sticks closer than a brother.

Proverbs 18:24

For he chose us in him before the creation of the world to be holy and blameless in his sight. In love he predestined us to be adopted as his sons through Jesus Christ, in accordance with his pleasure and will—to the praise of his glorious grace, which he has freely given us in the One he loves.

Ephesians 1:4-6

For the LORD will not forsake his people; he will not abandon his heritage; for justice will return to the righteous, and all the upright in heart will follow it.

Psalm 94:14-15 RSV

De Forest's Worthless Glass Bulb

Years ago in a federal courtroom in New York, a sarcastic district attorney presented to a jury a glass gadget which looked something like a small electric light bulb. With great scorn and ridicule, the attorney accused the defendant of claiming that this "worthless device" might be used to transmit the human voice across the Atlantic! He alleged that gullible investors had been persuaded by preposterous claims to buy stock in the company—an obvious act of fraud. He urged the jury to give the defendant and his two partners stiff prison terms. Ultimately, the two associates were convicted, but the defendant was given his freedom after he received a severe scolding from the judge.

The defendant was inventor Lee de Forest. The "worthless glass bulb" that was also on trial was the audion tube he had developed—perhaps the single greatest invention of the twentieth century. It was the foundation for what has became a multi-billion-dollar electronics industry.

No matter how harsh the criticism or how stinging the sarcasm aimed at your original ideas—pursue them further. Take them to their logical end, either convincing yourself that you were indeed wrong, or creating something new and beneficial!

Rejection

The poor and needy search for water, but there is none; their tongues are parched with thirst. But I the LORD will answer them; I, the God of Israel, will not forsake them.

Isaiah 41:17

Heal the sick, raise the dead, cleanse the lepers, cast out demons, freely you received, freely give.

Matthew 10:8 NAS

And Jesus said, "Neither do I condemn you; go your way. From now on sin no more."

John 8:11 NAS

He was despised and forsaken of men, a man of sorrows, and acquainted with grief; And like one from whom men hide their face, He was despised, and we did not esteem Him. Therefore I will allot Him a portion with the great, and He will divide the booty with the strong; because He poured out Himself to death, And was numbered with the transgressors; Yet He Himself bore the sin of many, And interceded for the transgressors.

Isaiah 53:3, 12 NAS

Use Your Resources

Sparky didn't have much going for him. He failed every subject in the eighth grade, and in high school, he flunked Latin, algebra, English, and physics. He made the golf team, but promptly lost the most important match of the season, and then lost the consolation match. He was awkward socially. While in high school, he never once asked a girl to go out on a date.

Only one thing was important to Sparky—drawing. He was proud of his artwork, even though no one else appreciated it. He submitted cartoons to the editors of his high school yearbook, but they were turned down. Even so, Sparky aspired to be an artist. After high school, he sent samples of his artwork to the Walt Disney studios. Again, he was turned down.

Still, Sparky didn't quit! He decided to write his own autobiography in cartoons. The character he created became famous worldwide—the subject not only of cartoon strips but countless books, television shows, and licensing opportunities. Sparky, you see, was Charles Schulz, creator of the "Peanuts" comic strip. Like his character, Charlie Brown, Schulz may not have been able to do many things. But rather than letting rejection stop him, he made the most of what he could do!

Relationships

A friend loves at all times.

Proverbs 17:17

Do not forsake your friend and the friend of your father.

Proverbs 27:10

If you are offering your gift at the altar and there remember that your brother has something against you, leave your gift there in front of the altar. First go and be reconciled to your brother; then come and offer your gift.

Matthew 5:23-24

Keep on loving each other as brothers.

Hebrews 13:1

Loyal Friends

Few sights evoke as much attention, and awe, as that of a large flock of Canadian geese winging their way in a V-formation to the north or south. They speak of the changing of seasons, and of the value of teamwork.

What many don't know is that when a goose becomes ill or wounded, it never falls from formation alone. Two other geese also drop out of formation and follow the ailing goose to the ground. One of them is usually the mate of the wounded bird, since geese mate for life and are extremely loyal to their mates. Once on the ground, the healthy birds help protect him and care for him as much as possible, even to the point of throwing themselves between the weakened bird and possible predators. They stay with him until he is either able to fly again, or dies. Then, and only then, do they launch out. In most cases, they wait for another group of geese to fly overhead and they join them, adding to the safety and efficiency of their numbers.

If only human beings would care for one another this well! Stick with your friends, and more importantly, stick by them.

Relationships

Children, obey your parents in the Lord: for this is right. Honour thy father and mother; which is the first commandment with promise; That it may be well with thee, and thou mayest live long on the earth.

Ephesians 6:1-3 KJV

Only be careful, and watch yourselves closely so that you do not forget the things your eyes have seen or let them slip from your heart as long as you live. Teach them to your children and to their children after them.

Deuteronomy 4:9

Marriage should be honored by all, and the marriage bed kept pure.

Hebrews 13:4

For the wife does not rule over her own body, but the husband does; likewise the husband does not rule over his own body, but the wife does.

1 Corinthians 7:4 RSV

On Being a "Sorrow-Carrier"

Although the North American Indians had
no written alphabet before they met the white
man, their language was anything but primitive.
The vocabulary of many Indian languages was as
large as that of their French and English
conquerors. Often, their expressions were far
more eloquent. In one Indian tongue, for
example, the word "friend" is beautifully stated as
"one-who-carries-my-sorrows-on-his-back."

A friend or family member who comes to
you for solace, or even asking for advice, often
wants nothing more than your presence, your
listening ear, and your quiet caring. A young man
discovered this shortly after his wedding. His new
bride frequently came home from work and told
him the woes of her day. His response was to
offer suggestions and give solutions to her
problems. His wife finally said to him, "I've
already solved the problems of the day." The
husband asked, perplexed, "Then why are you
telling me about them?" She replied, "I don't
need 'Mr. Fixit.' I need a loving ear."

A friend who provides both physical and
emotional shelter without always trying to fix
things is a true haven, one who helps another
weather the storms of life in safety.

Renewal

Do not conform any longer to the pattern of this world, but be transformed by the renewing of your mind. Then you will be able to test and approve what God's will is—his good, pleasing and perfect will.

Romans 12:2

Create in me a clean heart, O God; and renew a right spirit within me.

Psalm 51:10 KJV

Therefore if any man be in Christ, he is a new creature: old things are passed away; behold, all things are become new.

2 Corinthians 5:17 KJV

I will seek that which was lost, and bring again that which was driven away, and will bind up that which was broken, and will strengthen that which was sick.

Ezekiel 34:16 KJV

Transformation

Two friends who were in love with men who had deep-seated problems, decided to meet weekly to fast and pray. Over the weeks and months that followed, they prayed for every possible "angle" related to the difficulties their loved ones were experiencing. One of the women said, "We were praying for a *total* healing in their lives. Looking back, I realize we were also asking God to transform them into the men *we* thought they should be, and which we genuinely thought God wanted them to be."

After nearly a year, both of the women thought they had prayed all they could. "Nothing happened to improve our relationships," one of the women said. "Both men went their own way and we know of no change in their attitudes or behavior. What *did* happen was that my friend and I were transformed. *We* were healed of broken hearts and shattered dreams. *We* had our faith renewed and our hope restored. God surely will work in their lives, but the real miracle happened in us!"

When we pray for change in others, we may not get what we expect. As a result of spending time with God and caring for others enough to spend time praying on their behalf, we are changed.

Renewal

Cast away from you all the transgressions which you have committed against me, and get yourselves a new heart and a new spirit!

Ezekiel 18:31 RSV

Be made new in the attitude of your minds; and . . . put on the new self, created to be like God in true righteousness and holiness.

Ephesians 4:23-24

Brothers, I do not consider myself yet to have taken hold of it. But one thing I do: Forgetting what is behind and straining toward what is ahead, I press on toward the goal to win the prize for which God has called me heavenward in Christ Jesus.

Philippians 3:13-14

You have taken off your old self with its practices and have put on the new self which is being renewed in knowledge in the image of its Creator.

Colossians 3:9-10

Grow in Grace

The story is told of a king who owned a valuable diamond, one of the rarest and most perfect in the world. One day the diamond fell and a deep scratch marred its face. The king summoned the best diamond experts in the land to correct the blemish, but they all agreed they could not remove the scratch without cutting away a good part of the surface, thus reducing the weight and value of the diamond.

Finally one expert appeared and assured him that he could fix the diamond without reducing its value. His confidence was convincing, and the king gave the diamond to the man. In a few days, the artisan returned the diamond to the king, who was amazed to find that the ugly scratch was gone, and in its place a beautiful rose was etched. The former scratch had become the stem of an exquisite flower!

Any mistake we make in life may temporarily mar our reputation. But if we stick to what we know is right and continue to attempt to conform our will to that of God, we can trust Him to turn the "scratches" on our souls into part of His signature—that's what it means to grow in God's grace.

Restoration

Restore to me the joy of thy salvation, and uphold me with a willing spirit. The sacrifice acceptable to God is a broken spirit; a broken and contrite heart, O God, thou wilt not despise.

Psalm 51:12, 17 RSV

Restore us, O God; make your face shine upon us, that we may be saved.

Psalm 80:3

And the God of all grace, who called you to his eternal glory in Christ, after you have suffered a little while, will himself restore you and make you strong, firm and steadfast. To him be the power for ever and ever. Amen.

1 Peter 5:10-11

He restores my soul.

Psalm 23:3

Staying Together

Mike and Teri had one major thing in common: They both wanted to make their first million dollars by the age of thirty. Teri wasn't a Christian when they met, but Mike was; and after attending church with Mike and reading Christian books he gave to her, she accepted the Lord. They were married a short while later, and for the next two years lived what both called an ideal life.

Their focus on financial success, however, caused their dreams to unravel. They began to drift away from Jesus Christ, and away from each other. Eventually, they separated and divorced. A year after the divorce, Teri went to a conference and came away believing that God could restore their marriage. She began to pray earnestly for Mike.

Not long after, Mike began to recognize that God was not finished with him. He set his heart toward God, walked away from the life he had been leading, and made contact with Teri. They remarried and reordered the focus of their lives.

God is a God of restoration. When we place the broken pieces of our lives in His hands, He restores them to a beauty that far outshines the former.

Restoration

In the same way, I tell you, there is rejoicing in
the presence of the angels of God over one sinner
who repents.

Luke 15:10

Cast away from you all your transgressions,
whereby ye have transgressed; and make you a
new heart and a new spirit.

Ezekiel 18:31 KJV

But go and learn what this means: "I desire
mercy, not sacrifice." For I have not come to call
the righteous, but sinners.

Matthew 9:13

Repent ye therefore, and be converted, that your
sins may be blotted out, when the times of
refreshing shall come from the presence of
the Lord.

Acts 3:19 KJV

The Lord Is My Pacesetter

When we are in need of restoration in our lives, it is good to meditate on a favorite passage of Scripture. It reminds us of Who God is and what He will do for us. If you need restoration, consider this Japanese version of the twenty-third Psalm:

The Lord is my pacesetter . . .
I shall not rush

He makes me stop for quiet intervals

He provides me with images of stillness which restore my serenity

He leads me in the way of efficiency through calmness of mind and His guidance is peace

Even though I have a great many things to accomplish each day, I will not fret,

for His presence is here

His timelessness, His all importance will keep me in balance

He prepares refreshment and renewal in the midst of my activity by anointing my mind with the oils of tranquillity

My cup of joyous energy overflows

Truly harmony and effectiveness shall be the fruits of my hours

for I shall walk in the Pace of my Lord and dwell in his house for ever.

Shame

Fear not; you will no longer live in shame. The shame of your youth and the sorrows of widowhood will be remembered no more.

Isaiah 54:4 TLB

No one whose hope is in you will ever be put to shame, but they will be put to shame who are treacherous without excuse.

Psalm 25:3

May those who hope in you not be disgraced because of me, O LORD, the LORD Almighty; may those who seek you not be put to shame.

Psalm 69:6

See, I lay in Zion a stone that causes men to stumble and a rock that makes them fall, and the one who trusts in him will never be put to shame.

Romans 9:33

Down in the Mire

D. L. Moody told the story of a Chinese convert who gave this testimony:

> I was down in a deep pit crying for someone to help me out. As I looked up I saw a gray-haired man looking down at me. I said, "Can you help me out?" "My son," he replied, "I am Confucius. If you had read my books and followed what I taught, you would never have fallen into this dreadful pit." Then he was gone.

> Soon I saw another man coming. "My son," Buddha said, "forget about yourself. Get into a state of rest. Then, my child, you will be in a delicious state just as I am." "Yes," I said, "I will do that when I am above this mire. Can you help me out?" I looked and he was gone.

> I was beginning to sink into despair when I saw another figure above me. There were marks of suffering on His face. "My child," He said, "what is the matter?" But before I could reply, He was down in the mire by my side. He folded His arms about me and lifted. He did not say, "Shame on you for falling into that pit." Instead He said, "We will walk on together now."

Shame

Do your best to present yourself to God as one approved, a workman who does not need to be ashamed and who correctly handles the word of truth.

2 Timothy 2:15

Then, when that happens, we are able to hold our heads high no matter what happens and know that all is well, for we know how dearly God loves us, and we feel this warm love everywhere within us because God has given us the Holy Spirit to fill our hearts with his love.

Romans 5:5 TLB

Therefore being justified by faith, we have peace with God through our Lord Jesus Christ.

Romans 5:1 KJV

Rather, we have renounced secret and shameful ways; we do not use deception, nor do we distort the word of God. On the contrary, by setting forth the truth plainly we commend ourselves to every man's conscience in the sight of God.

2 Corinthians 4:2

The Parts of a Successful Life

Wallace E. Johnson, president of Holiday Inns and one of America's most successful builders, once said:

> I always keep on a card in my billfold the following verses and refer to them frequently: "Ask, and it shall be given you; seek, and ye shall find; knock, and it shall be opened unto you: for every one that asketh receiveth; and he that seeketh findeth; and to him that knocketh it shall be opened" (Matthew 7:7-8 KJV).

> These verses are among God's greatest promises. Yet they are a little one-sided. They indicate a philosophy of receiving but not of giving. One day as my wife, Alma, and I were seeking God's guidance for a personal problem, I came across the following verse which has since been a daily reminder to me of what my responsibility as a businessman is to God: "Study to shew thyself approved unto God, a workman that needeth not to be ashamed, rightly dividing the word of truth" (2 Timothy 2:15 KJV).

> Since then I have measured my actions against the phrase: "A workman that needeth not to be ashamed."

What standard do you measure your actions against?

Stewardship

The Lord answered, "Who then is the faithful and wise manager, whom the master puts in charge of his servants to give them their food allowance at the proper time? It will be good for that servant whom the master finds doing so when he returns.

Luke 12:42-43

Now it is required that those who have been given a trust must prove faithful.

1 Corinthians 4:2

Each one should use whatever gift he has received to serve others, faithfully administering God's grace in its various forms.

1 Peter 4:10

Good will come to him who is generous and lends freely, who conducts his affairs with justice.

Psalm 112:5

In the Service of Others

Oseola McCarty has spent most of her life helping people look nice—taking in bundles of dirty clothes, and washing and ironing them. She quit school in the sixth grade to go to work, never married, never had children, and never learned to drive because there was no place in particular she wanted to go. Her work was her life.

For most of her eighty-seven years, Oseola spent almost no money. She lived in her old family home, and bound her ragged old Bible with Scotch tape to keep the book of Corinthians from falling out. She saved her money, most of it coming in dollar bills and change, until she had amassed a little more than $150,000. That money became what people in Hattiesburg call "The Gift." She donated her entire savings—all $150,000—to black college students in Mississippi. She said, "I wanted to share my wealth with the children." Her great hope is to see a beneficiary of her gift graduate before she dies.

Oseola McCarty lived a life of stewardship and looked to the future, rather than to her own day-to-day needs. She will leave a legacy written on the hearts of grateful college graduates, who can perpetuate her generosity.

Stewardship

So then, men ought to regard us as servants of Christ and as those entrusted with the secret things of God.

1 Corinthians 4:1

And he sat down opposite the treasury, and watched the multitude putting money into the treasury. Many rich people put in large sums. And a poor widow came, and put in two copper coins, which make a penny. And he called his disciples to him, and said to them, "Truly, I say to you, this poor widow has put in more than all those who are contributing to the treasury. For they all contributed out of their abundance; but she out of her poverty has put in everything she had, her whole living."

Mark 12:41-44 RSV

Command those who are rich in this present world not to be arrogant nor to put their hope in wealth, which is so uncertain, but to put their hope in God, who richly provides us with everything for our enjoyment. Command them to do good, to be rich in good deeds, and to be generous and willing to share.

1 Timothy 6:17-18

Out of the most severe trial, their overflowing joy and their extreme poverty welled up in rich generosity. For I testify that they gave as much as they were able, and even beyond their ability. Entirely on their own, they urgently pleaded with us for the privilege of sharing in this service to the saints.

2 Corinthians 8:2-4

Investing the Best

On a December evening in 1995, the employees of Malden Mills in Lawrence, Massachusetts, thought their jobs had gone up in smoke. The mill had been destroyed by fire. But when morning came, the company leader, Aaron Feuerstein, told his 3,000-plus employees that he had decided to rebuild—immediately. Not only that, he intended to keep everyone on the payroll for thirty days.

It was not the first time Feuerstein had disregarded the obvious. When other textile mills in the area moved south to take advantage of lower taxes and cheaper labor, Feuerstein felt he had a responsibility to the people he employed, and stayed put.

When paychecks were handed out two days after the fire, each employee received a Christmas bonus and a note from the boss that read, "Do not despair. God bless each of you."

By January 2, the mill had reopened. Experts had said it could never be done. The mill was able to fill 80 percent of its orders in spite of the fire. Feuerstein's good stewardship of his employees and resources had been returned to him in miracle-working effort and loyalty.

When we give our best to others, we inspire them to give their best in return.

Strength

The LORD is my strength and song, and he is become my salvation: he is my God, and I will prepare him an habitation; my father's God, and I will exalt him.

Exodus 15:2 KJV

Trust in the LORD for ever, for the LORD God is an everlasting rock.

Isaiah 26:4 RSV

"My grace is sufficient for you, for my power is made perfect in weakness." Therefore I will boast all the more gladly about my weaknesses, so that Christ's power may rest on me.

2 Corinthians 12:9

Finally, my brethren, be strong in the Lord, and in the power of his might.

Ephesians 6:10 KJV

He'll Catch You

When Walter Wangerin was a boy, he told all of his friends that his father was the strongest man alive. Then came the day when Wally climbed to the top of the backyard cherry tree. A storm blew up suddenly and Wally was trapped. "Daddy!" he shouted, and instantly, his father appeared. "Jump," he yelled. "Jump, and I'll catch you."

Wally was frozen in fear. His big, strong dad looked quite small and frail down there on the ground, two skinny arms reaching out to catch him . Wally thought, *If I jump and Dad doesn't catch me, I'll hit the ground and die!* "No!" he screamed back. At that very moment the limb Wally was clinging to cracked at the trunk. Wally surrendered. He didn't jump—he *fell*—straight into Dad's ready arms. Crying and trembling, Wally wrapped his arms and legs around his father. Dad *was* strong after all. Up to that point, it had only been a theory. Now, it was a reality; it was *experience*.

Prayer is about surrendering our will to God's will, yielding our strength to God's strength, giving up our desires to take on God's desires, and surrendering when He asks us to jump into His waiting arms.

Strength

My flesh and my heart may fail, but God is the strength of my heart and my portion forever.

Psalm 73:26

You armed me with strength for battle; you made my adversaries bow at my feet.

2 Samuel 22:40

It is God that girdeth me with strength, and maketh my way perfect.

Psalm 18:32 KJV

He giveth power to the faint; and to them that have no might he increaseth strength.

Isaiah 40:29 KJV

Amazing Strength

A young man was running a race, and he found himself falling farther and farther behind his competitors. His friends cheered him on from the sidelines, but to no avail. Then suddenly, his lips began to move, his legs picked up speed, and to the amazement of the entire crowd watching the race, he passed his competitors one by one—and won the race!

After he had been awarded a blue ribbon and received the congratulations of his coach and teammates, he turned to his friends. One of them asked, "We could see your lips moving but we couldn't make out what you were saying. What were you mumbling out there?"

The young man replied, "Oh, I was talking to God. I told Him, 'Lord, You pick 'em up and I'll put 'em down. . . . You pick 'em up and I'll put 'em down!"

When we live our lives the way we know God's Word commands us, and we are believing to the best of our ability that the Lord will help us, we are then in a position to know with certainty what the Apostle Paul knew: "I can do all things through Christ which strengtheneth me" (Philippians 4:13 KJV).

Stress

You will keep in perfect peace him whose mind is steadfast, because he trusts in you. Trust in the LORD forever, for the LORD, the LORD, is the Rock eternal.

Isaiah 26:3-4

Drive out the mocker, and out goes strife; quarrels and insults are ended.

Proverbs 22:10

Rather, as servants of God we commend ourselves in every way: in great endurance; in troubles, hardships and distresses.

2 Corinthians 6:4

And seek the peace of the city whither I have caused you to be carried away captives, and pray unto the LORD for it: for in the peace thereof shall ye have peace.

Jeremiah 29:7 KJV

A Time for Rest

Our grandparents may have worked hard, with less sophisticated technology, but most analysts today agree that at the day's end, our grandparents gave themselves a chance to unwind. In today's world, there seems to be no downtime. The home has become a branch office—with cell phones in cars, beepers in pockets, and home offices complete with E-mail, fax machines, and answering machines waiting to be attended to. Some have estimated that more than 80 percent of all white-collar employees are in the habit of taking work home on a daily basis.

A report in *Newsweek* magazine quoted Dr. Mark Moskowitz of Boston University Medical Center as saying, "A lot of people are working twenty-four hours a day, seven days a week, even when they're not technically at work." Moskowitz sees this as a classic formula for first-class exhaustion. Stewart Noyce would probably agree. He is reported in the same magazine to have slept on his couch for an entire week, in a fit of exhaustion after graduating from business school. Noyce concluded, "It's really important to have some balance. Otherwise, it won't be fun anymore."

The writer of Ecclesiastes would no doubt say today, "There's a time for work . . . and for rest!"

Stress

LORD, you establish peace for us; all that we have
accomplished you have done for us.

Isaiah 26:12

Consider the blameless, observe the upright; there
is a future for the man of peace.

Psalm 37:37

Those who trust in the LORD are like Mount Zion,
which cannot be shaken but endures forever.

Psalm 125:1

And the peace of God, which passeth all
understanding, shall keep your hearts and minds
through Christ Jesus.

Philippians 4:7 KJV

Secret Prayer Warriors

Claire Townsend found the weekly production meetings at the major motion picture studio where she worked to be extremely stressful. All morning, various department heads would jockey for position. The studio had just been purchased, jobs were uncertain, and team spirit had vanished. To counteract the stress, Claire began to spend more time on her spiritual life. She began to pray again, discovering the power of God's love in her life. Even so, she dreaded this weekly battle.

Then one day during a particularly tense meeting, the thought came to her, *Pray. Pray now*. She began to imagine God's love pulsating within her, and then shooting out from her heart like a beam. She aimed her "love laser" toward the person sitting across from her. The coworker eyed her curiously and Claire smiled back. One by one, she beamed God's love to each person around the table as she silently prayed. Within minutes, the tone of the meeting changed from confrontation to compromise. As the group relaxed they became more creative, and Claire began to regard the meetings as an opportunity to impart God's love.

One of the best ways to counteract stress is through loving prayer for others.

Success

True humility and respect for the Lord lead a man to riches, honor and long life.

Proverbs 22:4 TLB

And, of course, it is very good if a man has received wealth from the Lord, and the good health to enjoy it. To enjoy your work and to accept your lot in life—that is indeed a gift from God.

Ecclesiastes 5:19 TLB

Riches and honor are with me, enduring wealth and prosperity. My fruit is better than gold, even fine gold, and my yield than choice silver.

Proverbs 8:18-19 RSV

Wealth and riches are in his house, and his righteousness endures forever.

Psalm 112:3

Fulfilling Your Purpose

At forty-three, Lenny felt the time had come to give something back to his community, so he volunteered at a feeding program for homeless people. Soon he was counseling the families who came for food, directing them to places that provided shelter and helping several of the men find jobs. The director of the program told him he had a talent for working with people and encouraged him to develop it.

Lenny had been working in a semi-clerical position as an administrative aide to a corporate executive. There wasn't any higher place he could go in his field. His one regret had been that he had never gone to college. Armed with the encouraging words of his fellow volunteers, he and his wife sold their home and went back to school. They both eventually earned doctoral degrees and became full-time family therapists. They opened a clinic together and rebuilt their lives, this time enjoying a much greater sense of personal fulfillment.

It's never too late to start a new career. And it's never too late to make a new start in your spiritual life. Genuine success is found in establishing a relationship with God, discovering who He created you to be, then developing talents and gifts He has given you!

Success

Then God will bless you with rain at planting time and with wonderful harvests and with ample pastures for your cows.

Isaiah 30:23 TLB

Then the LORD your God will make you most prosperous in all the work of your hands and in the fruit of your womb, the young of your livestock and the crops of your land.

Deuteronomy 30:9

The LORD will grant you abundant prosperity—in the fruit of your womb, the young of your livestock and the crops of your ground—in the land he swore to your forefathers to give you. The LORD will open the heavens, the storehouse of his bounty, to send rain on your land in season and to bless all the work of your hands. You will lend to many nations but will borrow from none.

Deuteronomy 28:11-12

He is like a tree planted by streams of water, which yields its fruit in season and whose leaf does not wither. Whatever he does prospers.

Psalm 1:3

Innovative Success

With only a high school diploma, Harlow Curtice landed a bookkeeper's job with a subsidiary of General Motors. Harlow, a country boy, rose to become a company president by age thirty-five. By the time he was forty, he had been appointed general manager of GM's prized Buick division.

Curtice made his way to the top of his profession with a flair for taking new ideas and putting them into action. He dared to design new styles and develop new models. Furthermore, he personally traveled throughout the United States to inspire dealers and instill in them a renewed enthusiasm for their Buick products.

The result? Even though his career was forged in the middle of the Depression, sales of Buick cars quadrupled! His division became the second biggest moneymaker in General Motors' history.

To what did Harlow Curtice attribute his success? He cited these three things:

1. He set goals for himself and required the same of the people around him;
2. He took pride in confronting and overcoming obstacles that blinded his vision; and
3. He was willing to do things losers refused to do. Therefore, winning became a habit!

By putting these principles into practice, you can develop the habit of winning.

Suffering

Blessed be God, even the Father of our Lord Jesus Christ, the Father of mercies, and the God of all comfort; Who comforteth us in all our tribulation, that we may be able to comfort them which are in any trouble, by the comfort wherewith we ourselves are comforted of God.

2 Corinthians 1:3-4 KJV

He was despised and rejected by men, a man of sorrows, and familiar with suffering. Like one from whom men hide their faces he was despised, and we esteemed him not.

Isaiah 53:3

I consider that our present sufferings are not worth comparing with the glory that will be revealed in us.

Romans 8:18

Thou therefore endure hardness, as a good soldier of Jesus Christ.

2 Timothy 2:3 KJV

Powerful Positive Response

When British minister W. E. Sangster first noticed an uneasiness in his throat and a dragging in his leg, he went to his physician. It was found that he had an incurable muscle disease that would result in gradual muscular atrophy until he died. Rather than retreat in dismay, Sangster threw himself into his work in British home missions. He figured he could still write and that he would have even more time for prayer. He prayed, "Lord, let me stay in the struggle. . . . I don't mind if I can no longer be a general." He wrote articles and books, and helped organize prayer cells throughout England. When people came to him with words of pity, he insisted, "I'm only in the kindergarten of suffering."

Over time, Sangster's legs became useless. He completely lost his voice. But at that point, he could still hold a pen and write, although shakily. On Easter morning just a few weeks before he died, he wrote a letter to his daughter, saying, "It is terrible to wake up on Easter morning and have no voice to shout, 'He is risen!'—but it would be still more terrible to have a voice and not want to shout."

Suffering

A righteous man may have many troubles, but the
LORD delivers him from them all.

Psalm 34:19

Yet if one suffers as a Christian, let him not be
ashamed, but under that name, let him glorify God.

1 Peter 4:16 RSV

Blessed is the man who perseveres under trial,
because when he has stood the test, he will receive
the crown of life that God has promised to those
who love him. When tempted, no one should say,
"God is tempting me." For God cannot be
tempted by evil, nor does he tempt anyone; but
each one is tempted when, by his own evil desire,
he is dragged away and enticed.

James 1:12-14

But join with me in suffering for the gospel, by
the power of God, who has saved us and called us
to a holy life—not because of anything we have
done but because of his own purpose and grace.

2 Timothy 1:8-9

In Every Circumstance

Max had one of the worst jobs in the camp—carrying stones and planks through the mud to build a crematorium. Daily, he was under the lash of the camp's infamous guard, "Bloody Krott." Yet all the while, Father Maximillian Kolbe kept smiling. One prisoner recalled, "Because they were trying to survive at any cost, all the prisoners had wildly roving eyes watching in every direction for trouble or the ready clubs. Kolbe, alone, had a calm straightforward look, the look of a thoughtful man. . . . In spite of his physical suffering, he was completely healthy, serene . . . extraordinary in character."

Kolbe often let others take his food ration. He said to those who questioned this, "Every man has an aim in life. Most of you men want to return to your wives . . . your families. My part is to give my life for the good of all men." Kolbe encouraged others to keep hope, to lift their voices in songs of praise. One recalled, "He made us see that our souls were not dead."

Good circumstances don't create great people. Great people create good in every circumstance.

Temptation

Be self-controlled and alert. Your enemy the devil prowls around like a roaring lion looking for someone to devour. Resist him, standing firm in the faith, because you know that your brothers throughout the world are undergoing the same kind of sufferings.

1 Peter 5:8-9

The Lord knows how to rescue godly men from trials and to hold the unrighteous for the day of judgment, while continuing their punishment.

2 Peter 2:9

Watch and pray so that you will not fall into temptation. The spirit is willing, but the body is weak.

Mark 14:38

Submit yourselves therefore to God. Resist the devil and he will flee from you.

James 4:7 RSV

Tempting Choices—Right Decisions

As college roommates, Meg and Ann became best friends. Then one day, Meg told Ann that John had asked her for a date. Ann was disappointed; she'd had a crush on John for two years. Still, she managed to say, "Have a good time" and later, to put on a happy face at John and Meg's wedding.

Through the years, Meg kept the relationship with Ann close. Ann enjoyed teasing and laughing with John. When Meg asked Ann to join them at a beachside bungalow for a week, Ann jumped at the chance. One afternoon when Meg went out to visit a friend, Ann and John betrayed Meg's trust. Afterward, Ann felt sick inside.

A few minutes of flirtation and passion resulted in more than a decade of misery for Ann. She might never have known happiness again if Meg hadn't confronted her about her refusal to accept a marriage proposal. Ann sobbed, "I'm horrible. You don't know how I've wronged you." Meg said, "I do know, Ann," and one look into her eyes confirmed that Meg had known, had loved, and had forgiven.

Temptation itself is not a sin, but allowing it to continue is. God always provides a way of escape; you must simply take it.

Temptation

No temptation has overtaken you that is not common to man. God is faithful, and he will not let you be tempted beyond your strength, but with the temptation will also provide the way of escape, that you may be able to endure it.

1 Corinthians 10:13 RSV

For since he himself has now been through suffering and temptation, he knows what it is like when we suffer and are tempted, and he is wonderfully able to help us.

Hebrews 2:18 TLB

And lead us not into temptation, but deliver us from evil: For thine is the kingdom, and the power, and the glory, for ever. Amen.

Matthew 6:13 KJV

Consider him who endured such opposition from sinful men, so that you will not grow weary and lose heart. In your struggle against sin, you have not resisted to the point of shedding your blood.

Hebrews 12:3-4

Temptation Defeated

As the ancient myth goes, when Ulysses sailed out to meet the Sirens, he stopped his ears with wax and had himself bound to the mast of his ship. He was apparently unaware that every traveler before him had done the same thing and that wax and chains were no match for the Sirens. Their alluring song could pierce through everything, causing sailors to break all manner of bonds.

The Sirens, however, had a more fatal weapon than their song. It was silence. As Ulysses approached them, the Sirens chose to employ that weapon. Rather than be seduced into straining to hear their song, however, Ulysses concluded that he alone must be the only person who could not hear their song and that he must be immune to their powers. Strengthened in that confidence, he set his gaze on the distant horizon and escaped the Sirens as no man before him.

Temptation always lies first in what we see and what we hear, then in what we choose to think on. Choose carefully where your eyes and ears wander, and temptation will be more easily defeated.

Thankfulness

Let your roots grow down into him and draw up nourishment from him. See that you go on growing in the Lord, and become strong and vigorous in the truth you were taught. Let your lives overflow with joy and thanksgiving for all he has done.

Colossians 2:7 TLB

And whatever you do or say, let it be as a representative of the Lord Jesus, and come with him into the presence of God the Father to give him your thanks.

Colossians 3:17 TLB

Thanks be to God, who gives us the victory through our Lord Jesus Christ.

1 Corinthians 15:57 NAS

Give thanks in all circumstances, for this is God's will for you in Christ Jesus.

1 Thessalonians 5:18

An Attitude of Gratitude

Fulton Oursler told a story of an old nurse who was born a slave on the eastern shore of Maryland. She had not only attended Fulton's birth, but that of his mother. He credits her for teaching him the greatest lesson he ever learned about thankfulness and contentment. Recalls Oursler:

> I remember her as she sat at the kitchen table in our house; the hard, old, brown hands folded across her starched apron, the glistening eyes, and the husky old whispering voice, saying, "Much obliged, Lord, for my vittles."
>
> "Anna," I asked, "what's a vittle?"
>
> "It's what I've got to eat and drink—that's vittles," the old nurse replied.
>
> "But you'd get your vittles whether you thanked the Lord or not."
>
> "Sure," said Anna, "but it makes everything taste better to be thankful."

For many people, poverty is not a condition of the pocketbook, but a state of mind. Do you think of yourself as being rich or poor today? What do you value and count as "wealth" in your life? If you are thankful for what you have, you are very wealthy indeed!

Thankfulness

Give thanks to the LORD, for he is good; his love endures forever. Let them give thanks to the LORD for his unfailing love and his wonderful deeds for men. Let them sacrifice thank offerings and tell of his works with songs of joy.

Psalm 107:1, 21-22

The LORD is my strength and my shield; my heart trusts in him, and I am helped. My heart leaps for joy and I will give thanks to him in song.

Psalm 28:7

Then he turned my sorrow into joy! He took away my clothes of mourning and gave me gay and festive garments to rejoice in so that I might sing glad praises to the Lord. . . . O Lord my God, I will keep on thanking you forever!

Psalm 30:11-12 TLB

Come, let us sing for joy to the LORD; Let us shout joyfully to the rock of our salvation. Let us come before His presence with thanksgiving; Let us shout joyfully to Him with psalms.

Psalm 95:1-2 NAS

Thou Shalt Not Whine

Here are four steps for turning whining into thanksgiving:

1. *Give something away.* When you give, you create both a physical and a mental space for something new and better to come into your life. Although you may think you are "lacking" something in life, when you give you demonstrate the abundance in your life.

2. *Narrow your goals.* Don't expect everything good to come into your life all at once. When you focus your expectations toward specific, attainable goals, you are more apt to direct your time and energy toward reaching them.

3. *Change your vocabulary from "I need" to "I want."* Most of the things we think we *need* are actually things we *want*. When you receive them, you will be thankful for even small luxuries, rather than seeing them as necessities you can't live without.

4. *Choose to be thankful for what you already have.* Thanksgiving is a choice. Every one of us has more things to be thankful for than we could even begin to recount in a single day.

As you put these steps into practice, you will find yourself whining less, and thanking God more. Living a life of gratitude and thanksgiving to God is the best antidote for stress there is!

Tragedy

The eternal God is a dwelling place, And underneath are the everlasting arms; And He drove out the enemy from before you, And said, "Destroy!"

Deuteronomy 33:27 NAS

Even when walking through the dark valley of death I will not be afraid, for you are close beside me, guarding, guiding all the way.

Psalm 23:4 TLB

When you pass through the waters, I will be with you; and when you pass through the rivers, they will not sweep over you. When you walk through the fire, you will not be burned; the flames will not set you ablaze.

Isaiah 43:2

I have told you these things, so that in me you may have peace. In this world you will have trouble. But take heart! I have overcome the world.

John 16:33

Deep Roots

Many people see abundant spring rains as a great blessing to farmers, especially if the rains come after the plants have sprouted and are several inches tall. What they don't realize is that even a short drought can have a devastating effect on a crop of seedlings that has received too much rain.

Why? Because during frequent rains, the young plants are not required to push their roots deeper into the soil in search of water. If a drought occurs later, plants with shallow root systems will quickly die.

We often receive abundance in our lives—rich fellowship, great teaching, thorough "soakings" of spiritual blessings. Yet when stress or tragedy enters our lives, we may find ourselves thinking God has abandoned us or is unfaithful. The fact is, we have allowed the "easiness" of our lives to keep us from pushing our spiritual roots deeper. We have allowed others to spoon-feed us, rather than develop our own deep personal relationship with God through prayer and study of His Word.

Only the deeply rooted are able to endure hard times without wilting. The best advice is to enjoy the "rain" while seeking to grow even closer to Him.

Tragedy

He heals the brokenhearted and binds up their wounds.

Psalm 147:3

Arise, shine; for your light has come, And the glory of the LORD has risen upon you. For behold, darkness will cover the earth, And deep darkness the peoples; But the LORD will rise upon you, And His glory will appear upon you.

Isaiah 60:1-2 NAS

For Thou hast been defense for the helpless, A defense for the needy in his distress, A refuge from the storm, a shade from the heat.

Isaiah 25:4 NAS

For I am convinced that nothing can ever separate us from his love. Death can't, and life can't. The angels won't, and all the powers of hell itself cannot keep God's love away. Our fears for today, our worries about tomorrow, or where we are— high above the sky, or in the deepest ocean— nothing will ever be able to separate us from the love of God demonstrated by our Lord Jesus Christ when he died for us.

Romans 8:38-39 TLB

Paths of Mercy and Truth

Beverly Sills has thrilled audiences with her beautiful operatic voice for years. Few people know, however, that her natural daughter was born deaf and that she has a stepdaughter who is also severely handicapped.

She writes in her autobiography, *Bubbles:*

I was now only thirty-four, but a very mature thirty-four. In a strange way my children had brought me an inner peace. The first question I had when I learned of their tragedies was self-pitying, "Why me?" Then gradually it changed to a much more important, "Why them?" Despite their handicaps they were showing enormous strength in continuing to live as normal and constructive lives as possible. How could Peter and I show any less strength?

Oscar Wilde once wrote: "In this world there are only two tragedies. One is not getting what one wants, and the other is getting it." A third tragedy may be added: the tragedy of not being able to go forward after tragedy has occurred. When a tragedy strikes, our first tendency is to ask "Why?" We may never know "why," but God promises to be with us always. When we make the decision to go on with life, He leads us on in His paths of mercy and truth.

Wisdom

If you want to know what God wants you to do, ask him, and he will gladly tell you, for he is always ready to give a bountiful supply of wisdom to all who ask him; he will not resent it.

James 1:5 TLB

The depth of the riches of the wisdom and knowledge of God! How unsearchable his judgments, and his paths beyond tracing!

Romans 11:33

Praise be to the name of God for ever and ever; wisdom and power are his. He reveals deep and hidden things; he knows what lies in darkness, and light dwells with him.

Daniel 2:20, 22

By wisdom the LORD laid the earth's foundations, by understanding he set the heavens in place.

Proverbs 3:19

Marking the Trouble Spots

Sara Orne Jewett has written a beautiful novel about Maine, *The Country of the Pointed Firs*. In it, she describes the path that leads a woman writer from her home to that of a retired sea captain named Elijah Tilley. On the way, there are a number of wooden stakes in the ground that appear to be randomly scattered on his property. Each is painted white and trimmed in yellow, just like the captain's house.

Once she arrives at the captain's abode, the writer asks Captain Tilley what the stakes mean. He tells her that when he first made the transition from sailing the seas to plowing the land, he discovered his plow would catch on many of the large rocks just beneath the surface of the ground. Recalling how buoys in the sea always marked trouble spots for him, he set out the stakes as "land buoys" to mark the rocks. Then he could avoid plowing over them in the future.

God's commandments are like buoys for us, revealing the trouble spots and rocky points of life. When we follow God's wisdom and steer clear of what is harmful to us, life is not only more enjoyable but more productive.

Wisdom

To the man who pleases him, God gives wisdom, knowledge and happiness.

Ecclesiastes 2:26

But we preach Christ crucified, a stumbling block to Jews and folly to Gentiles, but to those who are called, both Jews and Greeks, Christ the power of God and the wisdom of God. For the foolishness of God is wiser than men, and the weakness of God is stronger than men.

1 Corinthians 1:23-25 RSV

Where is the wise man? Where is the scribe? Where is the debator of this age? Has not God made foolish the wisdom of the world? For since in the wisdom of God the world through its wisdom did not come to know God, God was well-pleased through the foolishness of the message preached to save those who believe.

1 Corinthians 1:20-21 NAS

Because the foolishness of God is wiser than men, and the weakness of God is stronger than men. For consider your calling, brethren, that there were not many wise according to the flesh, not many mighty, not many noble; but God has chosen the foolish things of the world to shame the wise, and God has chosen the weak things of the world to shame the things which are strong.

1 Corinthians 1:25-27 NAS

Success Takes Wisdom

Charles Goodyear had no formal education. At the age of twenty-one, he went into partnership with his father in a hardware business that soon failed. It was the first of many losses. Failure and poverty characterized much of his life. His family frequently existed on the charity of neighbors. Six of his twelve children died in infancy. By the time he was forty, his health was very poor.

Most of Goodyear's troubles stemmed from his obsession with rubber. He had a fanatic determination to transform raw rubber into a useful material. To pursue his experiments, he sold his watch, the living room furniture, even the dishes off the table. Even while in jail, he experimented with rubber, trying to discover its unique properties and mold it to his satisfaction.

Quite by accident, he stumbled upon the process of vulcanizing rubber when he dropped a piece of the material that had been treated with sulfur on a hot stove. He refined this process, which opened the development of an entire industry. While he might have amassed a fortune, his own bad judgment resulted in his dying in poverty.

It takes more than effort and goals to gain *and keep* success. It also takes wisdom.

Work

Work hard and cheerfully at all you do, just as though you were working for the Lord and not merely for your masters, remembering that it is the Lord Christ who is going to pay you, giving you your full portion of all he owns. He is the one you are really working for.

Colossians 3:23-24 TLB

For even when we were with you, we gave you this rule: "If a man will not work, he shall not eat."
2 Thessalonians 3:10

If any man builds on this foundation using gold, silver, costly stones, wood, hay or straw, his work will be shown for what it is, because the Day will bring it to light. It will be revealed with fire, and the fire will test the quality of each man's work.
1 Corinthians 3:12-13

For I know the plans I have for you, says the Lord. They are plans for good and not for evil, to give you a future and a hope.
Jeremiah 29:11 TLB

Self-serve

One day, a grandfather told his grandchildren about his journey to America. He told of being processed at Ellis Island and how he had gone to a cafeteria in lower Manhattan to get something to eat. There, he sat down at an empty table and waited quite some time for someone to take his order. Nobody came. Finally, a woman with a tray full of food sat down opposite him and explained to him how a cafeteria works.

She said, "You start at that end"—pointing toward a stack of trays—"and then go along the food line and pick out what you want. At the other end, they'll tell you how much you have to pay."

The grandfather reflected a moment and then said, "I soon learned that's how everything works in America. Life's a cafeteria here. You can get anything you want—even very great success—if you are willing to pay the price. But you'll never get what you want if you wait for someone to bring it to you. You have to get up and get it yourself."

The difference between where you are and where you want to be can often be summed up in one word: work.

Work

When God gives any man wealth and possessions, and enables him to enjoy them, to accept his lot and be happy in his work—this is a gift of God.

Ecclesiastes 5:19

Do not work for food that spoils, but for food that endures to eternal life, which the Son of Man will give you.

John 6:27

God is not unjust; he will not forget your work and the love you have shown him as you have helped his people and continue to help them.

Hebrews 6:10

I will instruct you and teach you in the way you should go; I will guide you with My eye.

Psalm 32:8 NKJV

God's Work—God's Pay

As a young man, J. C. Penney ran a
butcher shop. He was told that if he gave a fifth
of Scotch to the head chef in a popular hotel, the
business of that hotel would be his. Penney did
this for some time. Then he felt convicted that
what he was doing was wrong. He discontinued
the gifts of liquor and sure enough, lost the
hotel's business, causing him to go broke. God,
however, had better things planned for him. In
time, he began a merchandise business that grew
into a nationwide enterprise.

Unsuccessful years alone don't create
success. Remaining true to principles and doing
the right thing—even when you seem to be
failing—produces success in time. A poem by an
unknown writer says it well:

> Who does God's work will get God's pay,
> However long may seem the day,
> However weary be the way;
> Though powers and princes thunder "Nay,"
> Who does God's work will get God's pay.
> He does not pay as others pay,
> In gold or land or raiment gay;
> In goods that vanish and decay;
> But God in wisdom knows a way,
> And that is sure, let come what may,
> Who does God's work will get God's pay.

Additional copies of this book and other titles
from Honor Books are available from
your local bookstore.

God's Little Book of Promises
God's Little Book of Promises for Mothers
God's Little Devotional Bible
God's Little Devotional Book series
God's Little Instruction Book series

Honor Books
Tulsa, Oklahoma